SOD'S LAW

Sam Leith was born in 1974. After a long series of other misfortunes, he found himself living in Archway, expecting a child, and out of a job. Before that he was the literary editor of the *Daily Telegraph*. He is now a freelance journalist. This is his second book. The first did terribly.

D062646 4

SOD'S LAW

Why Life Always Lands Butter Side Down

SAM LEITH

Atlantic Books
London

First published in paperback in Great Britain in 2009 by Atlantic
Books, an imprint of Grove Atlantic Ltd.

Copyright © Sam Leith 2009

1 2 3 4 5 6 7 8 9

A CIP catalogue record for this book is available from the British
Library.

ISBN: 978 1 84887 230 1

Illustrations by Henry Paker, © Henry Paker 2009

Printed in the UK by CPI Bookmarque, Croydon, CR0 4TD

Atlantic Books
An imprint of Grove Atlantic Ltd
Ormond House
26–27 Boswell Street
London
WC1N 3JZ

www.atlantic-books.co.uk

For my father – the most accident-prone man
I know, and without whom...

Contents

Introduction 1

A Note on Sources 10

THE PROFESSIONALS 13

SOD ON THE ROAD 25

THE COURSE OF TRUE LOVE 39

SOD'S WAR 47

OUT FOR A DUCK 63

SOD AND GOD 75

SOD AND PLOD 83

THE ART OF LOSING 97

SODDING POLITICS, SODDING POLITICIANS,
AND SODDING PUBLIC LIFE 119

THE QUEST FOR KNOWLEDGE 135

ODDS AND SODS 155

'*Tragedy* is when I cut my finger. *Comedy* is when you walk into an open sewer and die.'
— Mel Brooks

Introduction

'The devil farts in my face once more.'

When Edmund Blackadder spoke those words, he spoke for us all. He spoke for every explorer with his map upside down, for every air-traffic controller suddenly receiving Magic FM through his headphones, for every astronomer whose new planet turned out to be a bit of bran-flake on the eyepiece of his telescope.

In this age of doubt, fewer and fewer of us are prepared to believe that some supernatural agency gives a toss about our fate. Yet a belief in Sod's Law – the blind perversity of the inanimate – is everywhere. Search your soul. You have that belief. So did your ancestors, and so will your descendants.

If your descendants, that is, haven't died out or been herded into a cellar by cannibals as a direct result of the global apocalypse. Look about you, man. If ever the pale rider named Sod was in evidence, it's in the Year of Our Lord 2009, in the disaster-not-waiting-long-enough-to-happen that is Britain.

Ten years ago, we were on top of the world. We weren't at war with anyone, everyone had pots of money and everyone was sharing it about. It was great. One hundred per cent mortgage, sir? Come out from your cardboard box, put down that purple tin, and sign here. Yes, an X will do fine. Welcome to the property-owning democracy.

People started selling each other credit swap derivatives

and complexly securitized futures and hedges and God alone knows what else. Instead of asking what the bloody hell they thought they were doing – and while they were at it how come Iceland, which has nothing but fish and an old Björk album by way of assets, was richer on paper than the entire continent of Asia – we all went merrily along with it.

In due course, it turned out that all this money was completely made up: people were buying and selling worthless assets with imaginary money that they didn't own in the first place. And then – to the bafflement of simple-minded souls like myself who imagined that with a roughly stable amount of goods and services in the world, it can't be possible for EVERYONE to get poor at the same time – everyone got poor at the same time. Except for the man who owns Domino's Pizza.

We might as well have put a collection of chimps in charge of the global economy. At least they would have taken their bonuses in PG Tips.

Ah, I hear you say. Fortunately, we have the gold reserve to prop up our ailing currency. Except we bloody don't, because while he was Chancellor of the bloody Exchequer, Gordon bloody Brown sold 60 per cent of it for $275 an ounce – aka pottage, one mess of – while its price was at a twenty-year low. At the time of writing, gold is selling at $930 an ounce.

With a mind like that, it could only have been a matter of time before he became Prime Minister. But surely, I hear you say, nobody would vote an eejit like that into a position of power. And how right you are. Unfortunately, they didn't bloody need to.

I had a nice job, too. I used to be the Literary Editor – say it with capitals – of a respectable newspaper. Writers were nice to me at parties. People used to pretend they were interested in my opinions. Publicists pretended to find me attractive. Now I can barely get arrested.

No sooner had I decided that I was secure in my job, and had sorted myself out with a stonkingly enormous mortgage, a pregnant girlfriend, had spent most of my savings on a diamond ring and was halfway through planning the wedding, than I lost my job.

'Blah blah blah recession blah blah letting you go blah blah blah here's a black bin liner for your stuff can we have it back when you've finished?' was roughly how the conversation went.

Brilliant. Fortunately, I had something to fall back on. I had about £40,000 worth of shares, left to me by my late grandfather, God rest him.

Shares in HBOS.

So I'm now reduced to writing toilet books to keep my family from the poorhouse. Not that there's much chance of even that working. The last toilet book I wrote was a dismal failure in hardback – and when it was republished, completely redesigned and under an entirely different title, graduated to being a dismal failure in paperback.

And this from the publisher that sold a gazillion copies of *Life of Pi*: a perfectly absurd book about some kid named after a swimming pool sharing a boat with a tiger! I don't mind telling you I've changed publishers.

But I digress.

The fact is, Sod's Law appears in all cultures at all times. Socrates talked about 'the general cussedness of things'. His observation would have chimed with that of his near-contemporary Zeno, who committed suicide in 262 BC – and who can blame him? – after stubbing his toe.

The Anglo-Saxons said 'wyrd bith ful aræd' – which, freely translated, means: 'If there's a spare arrow flying around this battlefield you can bet your damn kingdom it's going to end up in my eye.'

The French, who were the beneficiaries on that occasion, call it 'la loi de l'emmerdement maximum' or, occasionally, 'la loi de la tartine beurrée'. The Germans use the phrase 'die Tücke des Objekts'.

Specialized instances are adduced and their statements refined and elaborated. 'The Peter Principle', for example, describes the aggregational effect of Sod's Law in the work-place ('in a hierarchy, every employee tends to rise to the level of his incompetence'). 'Muphry's Law' states, correctly, that anything you write criticizing a piece of proofreading will contain a spelling mistake. Other corollaries and off-shoots, such as 'the Buggeration Factor' or 'Finagle's Law', continue to be the subject of detailed scholarly disputes.

Whatever its guise, we all know it when we see it. Its founding principle, the axiom from which all the others proceed, is this: if anything can go wrong, it surely will.

'Sod's Law' is glossed with three citations in the *Oxford English Dictionary*. They are from an October 1970 issue of the *New Statesman*, from a September 1978 issue of the *New Scientist*, and from the July 1980 issue of *SLR Camera* magazine. Only the third bears quotation.

'Even if you're using a masking frame this can easily over-balance. According to Sod's Law, that's going to happen when you're halfway through exposing a sheet of 20 x 16 inch colour paper costing the best part of £1.30.'

I have no idea what those two sentences are talking about, but I am interested to see that 'over-balance' is hyphenated rather than all one word.

In March 2009, *Viz* – if the *OED* can include citations from periodicals, so can I – defined a special case of Sod's Law it called 'Chod's Law, n.': 'The axiomatic principle that, when having a quiet day at home watching *Cash in the Attic*, repeats of *Top Gear* and *Ice Road Truckers*, at the point at which you decide to go for a shit, find yourself an *Auto Trader* [editor's note: *Viz* magazine has immemorially associated *Auto Trader* magazine with defecation] and sit down for a leisurely half hour on the pot, no sooner have your cheeks touched plastic than the bloody phone rings, the fucking meter reader knocks on the door or some bastard tries to deliver a parcel.'

If you look up Murphy's Law in the *OED*, on the other hand, the entry tells you: 'see Murphy, n.' Turn, pilgrim, to 'Murphy, n.' You will be informed: 'Slang. A potato.' At this point you will make 'Murphy's face, n.'

This is a rare instance of Murphy's Law acting reflexively. Or, taken along with the bizarre fragment from a long-forgotten issue of *SLR Camera*, it is proof positive that the lexicographers were slightly on the skive that day.

Unsurprisingly, Wikipedia isn't much help either. Wikipedia is, after all, no more than a sophisticated tool for ensuring that Sod's Law maximally contaminates the global information supply.

Here, for example, is an extract from a scholarly discussion on the entry for 'Finagle's Law', aka 'Finagle's Law of Dynamic Negatives', aka 'Finagle's Corollary to Murphy's Law'.

The difference is that Murphy's Law is (or was originally) supposedly much more specific than what most people cite as Murphy's Law. What most people call Murphy's Law is actually Finagle's Law, and despite the name, Finagle's Law doesn't follow from the specific version of Murphy's Law. On the other hand, the Murphy's Law article is already about Finagle's Law, and the original statement of Murphy's

> Law is now little more than a footnote in the public mind. In a non sequitur, Hanlon's Razor has little or nothing to do with Murphy, Finagle, or either of their Laws, so I'm going to take that out.

WTF?, as the young people say. Thank you, Proginoskes, anyway, whoever you are.

There was a real Murphy, though. While Arthur Bloch was compiling his 1977 treatise on Murphy's Law for publication, he received at the eleventh hour a letter from one George Nichols of South Carolina.

Mr Nichols, who had been the Reliability and Quality Assurance Manager of a Nasa jet propulsion lab, attested that the phrase originated from Air Force Project MX981 at Edwards Air Force Base in California.

MX981 involved strapping crash-test dummies, chimpanzees and a brave fellow named Captain John Paul Stapp to a rocket-sled and seeing what happened to them when the speeding rocket-sled – nicknamed the 'Gee Whiz' – stopped abruptly, subjecting its cargo to pressures of anything up to forty-six times the force of gravity. The photographs of what happened to Stapp are worth looking up.

Captain Edward Aloysius Murphy, Jr (1918–1990) was a reliability engineer who arrived at Edwards armed with some 'strain gauges'. These devices were designed to measure more accurately the g-forces involved in Stapp's face-squelching encounters with rocket-powered deceleration.

The first time he tried them, the readings came out stone blank. The strap transducers had been put in backwards. Murphy blamed one of his assistants. 'If there's any way they can do it wrong, they will,' he said (according, at least, to one version of the story).

This was later refined into the simpler formulation

familiar to us now. When Stapp was asked at a press conference why no serious harm had come to anyone in the course
of all these crazed rocket-sled experiments, he explained that
the researchers had taken careful account of 'Murphy's Law'
as they went about their business.

Captain Murphy, apparently, was not as pleased by his
fame he might have been. Convinced that he had in fact
crystallized a vital principle of defensive design, he regarded
– according to public statements by his son – the commonplace interpretation of his dictum as 'ridiculous, trivial and
erroneous'. That is, of course, the law in operation.

But there's more in all this than malfunctioning strap
transducers. Consider the big picture. The existence of Sod's
Law, and the existence of our unfailing belief in it, invites
us to consider some of the most serious issues – not only
about the heroic perversity of the universe, but about human
self-obsession.

The less convinced we are that a personal deity has a
grand plan for us, the more convinced we are that the
invisible order of the universe is conspiring to make our
toast land butter side down. This vestigial determinism – is it
hard-wired into our brains? – is on the face of it egomaniacal.

If it's self-obsessed to think that some unearthly power is
directing the eventual well-being of our immortal souls, it's
immeasurably more self-obsessed to think that a similar
power is working, with unblinking eye and unfailing attention, to spoil our breakfasts. Slightly.

How alarming, though, to come to the realization that
this isn't simply a product of human delusion: we're right.
Just because you're paranoid, as the man said, doesn't mean
that they're not out to get you. The invisible order of the
universe really is conspiring to make your toast land butter
side down – and no less an organ than the *European Journal*

of Physics has confirmed it.

The buttered toast problem is one of the textbook manifestations of Sod's Law. It has been, as a consequence, subject to systematic scientific scrutiny. The breakthrough came in 1995, when Robert Matthews of Aston University, Birmingham, turned his attention to the problem.

Matthews – a theoretician of some rigour – was unsatisfied with the quality of previous experiments on the subject. He singled out as 'dynamically inappropriate', for instance, a 1993 edition of the BBC's popular science programme *QED*, which had attempted to gather data on the problem by having lab technicians toss buttered bits of bread up in the air and see how they landed. 'Hardly common practice around the breakfast table,' he remarked, witheringly. *QED*'s conclusion – that toast landed butter side down only about half the time – was accordingly dismissed.

Matthews set out, rather, to diagram the actual physics of falling toast. He modelled the tasty breakfast food familiar to us all 'as a thin, rigid, rough lamina', and managed to formulate an equation demonstrating that from a table of average height, there will be insufficient gravitational torque induced in the falling toast to turn it a full circle in the air.

This was expressed in the equation: if $wT + O < 270$, the toast lands butter side down – where w is the angular velocity of the toast, T is the time it spends falling, and O is the slight angle at which it leaves the table. Effectively, what this says, is that the toast needs to spin more than 270° in the air to have a chance of landing butter side up.

And Matthews demonstrates that from no table that a human might sensibly use, would that magic 270° of rotation be likely. Our tables would need to be three metres tall.

From this, he draws his truly startling conclusion. The way the toast lands is dictated by the maximum height of the breakfast table. The maximum height of the breakfast table is dictated by the maximum height of a human being. And the maximum height of a human being is dictated by three of the 'fundamental constants of the universe': the electromagnetic fine structure constant, the gravitational fine structure constant, and the Bohr radius.

These constants date back to the Big Bang. Ergo, Matthews concludes in his awe-inspiring paper, it is written into the very nature of the universe that your toast will fall butter side down.

Murphy gave it a name, and Sod gave it a tone of voice. But the law is as old as the universe itself. Indeed, probably older. In this, it resembles God – Who is in all places at all times, Whose existence man infers through the workings of His creation, towards an understanding of Whom man continues to grope blindly, and to Whom man has given countless names over the years but Whose essential attributes remain ineffable.

Sod, also, moves in mysterious ways. It seems quite plausible to me that the global history of religious observance was, at root, a mix-up or a mishearing. Indeed, given that The Word Was With God and The Word Was God – who's to say the Word was spelt correctly?

These are matters to ponder.

SL, London, June 2009

A Note on Sources

In assembling this book I have taken little or no care to ensure that the stories I include are true. I have tended, rather, to take the view that their cautionary force is undiminished by not all having, *per se*, exactly, HAPPENED, so to speak.

My chief concern, rather, was that the reader of these stories would come away a little wiser or a little happier for knowing them. Not all truth is literal truth. But all of the stories in this book were at some point or another earnestly believed to be true, and in almost all cases still are.

I haven't made any of these up.

I do not doubt, though, that the odd urban legend has slipped through the net. Can the guide dog who lost four owners really have been called 'Lucky'? Was Tithonus a real guy? My criterion in each case has been that the more funny or poignant a story was, the more I decided it was true.

I also owe a debt of thanks to some distinguished predecessors – authors like Christopher Logue, Sophocles, Stephen Pile, Sheridan Morley, John Gross, Hugh Vickers and the countless bloggers who swap candidates for Darwin Awards. Their various researches, while not covering identical terrain (where astonishing bad luck ends, and pinheaded stupidity or culpable uselessness begins, is a matter for debate), often overlap with my own.

I have whipped the funnier and more perverse anecdotes

from their work. My excuse for this is that these books all purport to be collections of true stories, most of them in the public domain. If it turns out that one or other of these individuals, in a shocking imposture on their reading public, did in fact make their stories up, and now sues me for breach of copyright...

Well, that would be just my sodding luck.

SL, London, June 2009

THE PROFESSIONALS

In April 1995, the janitor of Carroll Fowler Elementary School in Ceres, California was presented with a gopher that had been captured in the school grounds. Gophers being regarded, in California, not as cute children's television presenters but verminous nuisances, he set about trying to find a way to kill it humanely.

When he couldn't think of one, he and two colleagues hauled the beast into a small store cupboard, and started spraying it in the face with an aerosol cleaner designed to freeze chewing gum off pavements.

The gopher placidly blinked its way through three full cans of this stuff before they gave up. It seemed quite unharmed. The janitor lit a cigarette while he figured out what to do next, and the fume-filled cupboard did what any fume-filled cupboard will do when you light a cigarette in it.

The explosion hospitalized all three men and injured sixteen children who were passing through its blast radius on their way to morning assembly. The gopher was found, again quite unharmed, blinking placidly from a nearby wall.

It was released into the wild.

* * *

A crew of soldiers – filling in during the UK firefighters' strike of 1978 – was called out by an old lady in suburban south

London to rescue her cat from a tree. This they did with complete success, earning the lady's undying gratitude. As they reversed their fire engine out of her drive, they ran the cat over.

* * *

Along with the usual collection of rusty bicycles, vandalized scooters and fugitive shopping trolleys, workers dredging the rubbish out of a murky stretch of the Chesterfield–Stockwith canal in 1978 pulled out what appeared to be a giant plug of ancient design. It was only a couple of hours until – following reports of a mysterious 'whirlpool' – the canal vanished altogether.

* * *

The following is a fragment from an Internet chat room, archived at www.bash.org.

> *<Ben174>: If they only realized 90% of the overtime they pay me is only cause i like staying here playing with Kazaa when the bandwidth picks up after hours.*
> *<ChrisLMB>: If any of my employees did that they'd be fired instantly.*
> *<Ben174>: Where u work?*
> *<ChrisLMB>: I'm the CTO at LowerMyBills.com*
> **** Ben174 (BenWright@TeraPro33-41.LowerMyBills.com) Quit (Leaving)*

* * *

The laws of nature can often bring their victims into conflict with the laws of man. A prime example is that of 67-year-old Ronald Moore, arraigned in a Hastings magistrate's court for parking his car on a zebra crossing.

He was released after he explained that he would never have committed the offence 'if I hadn't run myself over in my own car the previous day'. After his automatic garage door had failed to open, he explained, he got out of his car to open them manually, in the course of which expedition he got his artificial leg wedged in a grating.

The car, whose handbrake he had failed to engage, rolled back and ran him over, crushing his artificial leg into what he later described as 'a U-shape' and severely bruising his real one. Wedged under the car, Mr Moore was not rescued for several hours and could barely walk after his ordeal.

'The leg repair shop is in the centre of town,' he explained, 'and that's why I parked on the zebra crossing.' The beak let him off.

* * *

The newsreader and cat lover Martyn Lewis (b. Swansea, 1945) claimed in 1993 that the media should make more of an effort to report good news, rather than the depressing alternative. This is not the policy of this book, evidently, but we salute Mr Lewis for trying.

Sod's Law, of course, ensured that all subsequent coverage of Mr Lewis's personal trials would be couched in tones of startlingly heartless jocularity ('Martyn Lewis, the television presenter most famous for his campaign to give viewers only good news, has been privately suffering an agonizing family tragedy.' *Daily Mail*, 13 April 2004).

The question is: was Mr Lewis on to something?

'196,459,483 Citizens Were Not Killed in Auto Accidents

this Year,' was one of the headlines in the closing issue of *Good News*, an *avant-la-lettre* experiment in putting into practice the principles Mr Lewis was to make famous.

Good News was a bi-weekly newspaper that, from its head-quarters in Sacramento, published cheering stories ('Fantastic Drop in Suicide Rate'; 'No War Declared in Sixteen Weeks'; 'Triple Rapist Enters Monastery') to the inhabitants of all fifty American states.

It ceased trading after sixteen months. Its final issue carried no report of its closure, said its founder, as 'such an item would have been against our policy'.

* * *

More Internet chat, archived at www.bash.org:

> *<Rabidplaybunny87>: Okay, so my neighbors officially hate me*
> *<GarbageStan23>: why?*
> *<Rabidplaybunny87>: Well, me, david and andrew were having a bonfire in the backyard, and we were making s'mores and all... and suddenly we here sirens, and see a firetruck turn into the street in front of us.*
> *<Rabidplaybunny87>: So we all went running to see what was up, and our neigbor's house was on fire!*
> *<GarbageStan23>: oh shit!*
> *<Rabidplaybunny87>: Yeah, and when we got there, the wife was crying into her husbands arms, and we were just kinda standing there, and then she saw us, and then like for 10 seconds, gave us the dirtiest look ever*
> *<Rabidplaybunny87>: Turns out, we were still holding our sticks with marshmallows on it, watching the fire...*

* * *

Eleanor Barry, a Broadway actress, took immense pride in the newspaper clippings she collected throughout her career. In 1977 she was found dead in her New York apartment at the age of 70, having been crushed to death by a pile of her scrapbooks.

* * *

Around the middle of the last century, so the story goes, the managing editor of one of Britain's national newspapers was trawling through the ledgers when he noticed that the newspaper was, every month, paying a substantial retainer to a correspondent in a part of the world the late Alan Clark would have referred to as Bongo-Bongo Land. He had never heard of this correspondent. A trawl through the cuttings library established that nor had anybody else: the last time this man's byline had appeared on a dispatch was in the previous decade.

The foreign editor was instructed to find out what was up.

He sent a telegram: 'WHY UNFILE'

With surprising promptness, the reply came back: 'UNFILE UNSTORY'

He sent another telegram: 'UNSTORY UNJOB'

The reply came: 'UPSTICK JOB ARSEWISE'

* * *

Erratum slip from *Wines and Spirits* by L. W. Marrison: 'Coates & Co. (Plymouth) Ltd, the sole makers of Plymouth Gin, point out that the special flavour is in no way due to the use of sulphuric acid. The author and publishers regret the inaccurate statements to the contrary which appear on page 252.'

* * *

In the autumn of 2008, Swansea Council set out to discourage big lorries from using a narrow road near the Morriston branch of Asda.

In order to do their duty by the Welsh-speaking community, the council emailed their translation service to ask what 'No Entry For Heavy Goods Vehicles. Residential Site Only' is in Welsh.

Back came the reply and in due course, on the junction between Clase and Pant-y-Blawd roads, they erected a large metal sign. Underneath the English text were the words: 'Nid wyf yn y swyddfa ar hyn o bryd. Anfonwch unrhyw waith i'w gyfieithu,' which is Welsh for 'I am not in the office at the moment. Send any work to be translated.'

This isn't the first Anglo-Welsh municipal translation failure, and nor will it be the last. In 2006 signage on a cycle path outside Cardiff warned cyclists of the dangers of an 'inflamed bladder', and – in a life-imperilling riposte to the signpost-twisting antics of the Welsh nationalists – a pedestrian crossing in Cardiff invited English speakers to 'look right' and Welsh speakers to 'look left'.

* * *

Unemployed plumber Fred Brooks, 46, sought to do a good deed when on his own initiative he prised up a Georgia manhole cover and jumped down it to see if he could clear a blocked sewer. He did the job, and headed back to the surface, poking his head out of the manhole just in time to be fatally beaned by a passing car.

* * *

It is through the *Memoirs* of the pocket-sized Anglo-Irish poetess Laetitia Pilkington that we know much of what we know about the personal habits of the satirist Jonathan Swift. A friend and disciple forty years his junior, her obedient attendance on him is an object demonstration of the maxim that no good deed goes unpunished.

Mrs Pilkington and her husband Matthew were described by Dean Swift as 'a little young poetical parson who has a little young poetical wife'. On making their acquaintance the great man of letters lost no time securing Matthew a post hundreds of miles away in London, and being ungallant to his wife.

At Christmas dinner one year, Swift put the wine bottle by the fire so the pitch that was used to seal the cork melted, then smeared the black sticky goo all over her face. Mrs Pilkington said something gracious about how honoured she was that he 'sealed her for his own'. Determined to get a rise, Swift asked volubly whether anyone had ever seen 'such a dwarf' as Pilkington, before demanding she take off her shoes so he could measure her up against the wainscot.

This he did by pushing down on her head – she was pregnant at the time, his biographer Victoria Glendinning tells us – so hard she crumpled in half. 'Making a mark with a pencil,' Laetitia tells posterity, 'he affirmed that I was but three feet two inches high.' She was in such pain she couldn't eat her meal.

On another occasion, she was summoned to the Deanery first thing in the morning. Swift, feeling like a spot of break-fast, demanded she open the bottom drawer in his cabinet and get out a bottle of rum.

Laetitia bent down to try and open the drawer, and couldn't do so. Immediately, the man of God started setting about her with his fists.

'I once again made an effort,' she recalled, 'and still he beat me, crying "Pox take you! Open the drawer!" I once more tried, and he struck me so hard that I burst into tears, and said, "Lord, sir, what must I do?" "Pox take you for a slut!" said he. "Would you spoil my lock and break my key?"'

Laetitia at last managed to explain that the drawer was locked.

'Oh!' said Swift. 'I beg your pardon.'

* * *

In the autumn of 2008, the editors of *MaxPlanckForschung*, the journal of the Max Planck Institute, one of Germany's most prestigious research bodies, published a special issue dedicated to China. They asked one of their journalists to find 'an elegant Chinese poem' to adorn the cover, and he duly came up with five columns of pretty-looking pictograms, which they printed in elegant white on red.

Only when the issue fell into the hands of native Chinese speakers did it become clear that something had gone wrong. The literal translation of the 'poem' was as follows:

> With high salaries, we have cordially invited for an extended series of matinees K. K. and Jiamei as directors, who will personally lead jade-like girls in the spring of youth,
> Beauties from the north who have a distinguished air of elegance and allure,
> Young housewives having figures that will turn you on;
> Their enchanting and coquettish performance will begin within the next few days.

'It is not my intention to provide a complete *explication de texte*,' wrote linguistics blogger Victor Mair in a thoughtful post-mortem. He was prepared to venture, though, that it appeared to be an advertisement for some form of adult entertainment.

'Regardless of how we interpret the quadripartite character,' Mair mused, 'we can tell from the context that it indicates the two individuals who are in charge of the girls in the show. Clearly this is an advertisement for some kind of burlesque business. I did find quite a few references on the web to a "K. K. Juggy" from a group called "Machine Gun Fellatio", and apparently the K. K. in her name stands for "Knickers" and "Knockers". Perhaps K. K. in the sense of "Knickers and Knockers" is an Australian expression, since K. K. Juggy (Christa Hughes) is from Sydney.'

And there, perhaps, the mystery is best left.

* * *

When it opened in 1904, the London Coliseum was the grandest playhouse of its day – costing £300,000, it was the apple of the impresario Oswald Stoll's eye.

It was designed with a giant revolving stage, so that scene changes could be effected in the very blinking of an eye. And – to impress the King and Queen – they installed a sort of horizontal elevator, sybaritically outfitted, which would carry the royal party on rails from the theatre entrance to the Royal Box without taxing the fat King's legs.

Immediately on entering the Theatre, the Royal party will step into a richly furnished lounge, which, at a signal, will move softly along a track formed in the floor, through a salon into a large foyer, which contains the entrance to the

> Royal Box. The Lounge-Car remains in position at the
> entrance to the Box and serves as an ante-room during the
> performance.

So, at least, boasted the programme for the opening night.
What it should more accurately have said was:

> Immediately on entering the Theatre, the Royal party will
> step into a richly furnished lounge, which, at a signal, will
> shudder a few feet forward, emit an anguished groan as
> from the bowels of hell, and grind to a complete halt,
> stranding their Gracious Majesties halfway between St
> Martin's Lane and the Crush Bar.

'Tum-Tum' – as Edward VII was known behind his broad
back – had to complete the short waddle to the Royal Box on
foot.

Flushed with the success of this, Stoll thought further to
please the King with an even more ambitious entertainment.
He would stage an indoor re-enactment of the King's
favourite sporting event, the Epsom Derby, live at the
Coliseum with the horses galloping on the spot, hamster-
wheel-style, against the direction of his revolving stage.

It takes a particular sort of genius to hit on a scheme like
this, and what any normal person can see would happen
happened. One of the horses promptly went flying off the
stage and crashed into the orchestra pit, squashing its unfortunate jockey flat and severely injuring the string section.

SOD ON THE ROAD

In summer 2008, a Syrian truck driver named Necdet Bakimci set out to drive his 32-ton car transporter from Antakya, near the Syrian border in Turkey, to Gibraltar off southern Spain.

Trusting to satnav, he stopped to ask directions only when his truck finally got stuck in a narrow country lane. He had arrived at the Gibraltar Point nature reserve near Skegness, Lincolnshire, 1,600 miles away from his intended destination.

* * *

During the Iran-Contra affair in 1986, Oliver North – a bumbler among bumblers – organized a diplomatic mission to Tehran. The idea was that relations with the regime would be improved by his delivery in person of a shipment of spare parts for Hawk missiles, in exchange for which the regime would arrange for Hezbollah to release American hostages held in Beirut.

Ollie and his companion, National Security Adviser Robert McFarlane, brought with them a couple of gifts designed to oil the wheels of diplomacy. They duly presented this devout Islamic regime with a Bible signed by Ronald Reagan, and an enormous chocolate cake. The cake might have been delicious, but since their visit came in the middle of Ramadan, their hosts could only stare at it and drool. Written on the bottom of the chocolate cake was 'a present from Tel Aviv'.

* * *

No book on misfortune could be complete without a tip of the hat to Larry Walters, the American truck driver who embodied all the most go-ahead characteristics of that proud body of men.

On 2 July 1982, on the roof of his girlfriend's house in San Pedro, California, 33-year-old Mr Walters strapped himself into a parachute, and tested out for the first time the invention he called 'Inspiration I' – an invention that would help him fulfil his lifelong dream of flight.

'Inspiration I' was an ordinary garden chair, to which Mr Walters had tied forty-five helium-filled weather balloons. He further equipped himself with a large bottle of fizzy drink, a pellet gun, thirty-five milk jugs full of water (for 'ballast'), a CB radio, an altimeter and a camera.

His notion was – once his friends had cut the chair's tethers – to ascend at a gentle rate, and then drift with the wind across the Mojave desert towards the Rocky Mountains at a height of 300 feet or so. When he wanted to descend, he would use his pellet gun to pop a couple of balloons and bring him drifting back to earth.

Unfortunately, the house's sharp roof abruptly severed one of the tethers, and before Larry and his friends had the chance to adjust the ballast/helium ratio, he was shooting directly upwards at more than a thousand feet per minute.

He was at 16,000 feet when the pilot of a TWA jetliner radioed the control tower to report a man in a garden chair floating through the main approach corridor to Los Angeles International Airport.

After a couple of hours of drifting in the freezing air – the view, he said afterwards, was so lovely that he hadn't remembered to take a single photograph – Larry plucked up courage to start popping the balloons. As he fell to earth, he crashed into a power line and blacked out Long Beach. He was unharmed.

'We know he broke some part of the Federal Aviation Act,' a police spokesman reportedly said after his arrest, 'and as soon as we decide which part it is, some type of charge will be filed.'

* * *

A delegation of 250 of those underappreciated idealists, the British Communist Party, decided in 1979 to travel to Calais to march in protest against the Common Market.

Why communists would want to protest against the Common Market is a point worth wondering about. You'd think that, disagreeable as the 'market' part would seem to them, the 'common' part of the phrase, and the essentially international character of the endeavour, would somehow cancel it out and leave them apathetic on the subject. No matter. They objected; they travelled; and they travelled alas in vain.

When they arrived they discovered that the jazz band that was supposed to be at the head of the march (again, you have to wonder about what on earth they thought a jazz band had to do with anything) wasn't coming after all. Also, they had left their banners on the coach at Dover. Judging that being English, and having no banners, would make their march somewhat unintelligible to the onlookers they hoped to stir with revolutionary resolve, they decided to abandon the march proper, and instead have a sort of mini-march from lunch to the meeting hall.

This was abandoned because the meeting hall turned out to be across the road from where they were having lunch. They discovered, further, that while they were eating they had missed the international meeting of trade unionists they'd planned to join, and that the proposed reception with the mayor of Calais had been called off because the venue had been double-booked by a convention of football referees.

* * *

It is courtesy of the unrivalled gossip site Popbitch that I became aware of the misfortune that befell Richi Abarca, singer in the Mexican teen band Magneto, a few years back.

Magneto had arrived in Guatemala City by helicopter, and were met at the airport by hordes of fans. As Richi stepped off the helicopter he raised his hands to greet the crowd. Unfortunately – Richi being only 16 years old, and dumb as a stump – the rotor blades were still going round.

Three of his fingers were found, spread out over a hundred-metre radius. His index and middle fingers were reattached and are making a full recovery, though the restoration of his little finger proved only a partial success. Richi's ring finger is still missing.

* * *

Brian Thompson's *Imperial Vanities* tells the story of Sam Baker, a doughty nineteenth-century colonist determined to build himself a farm in the inhospitable uplands of Ceylon. 'Things,' Thompson writes in a sentence designed to gladden our hearts, 'began badly.'

His daughter Jane died at sea on the passage from Mauritius
and the toddler son on whom he doted was poisoned by a
servant shortly after he set foot on Ceylon. The argosy from
England arrived safely enough, but trouble began immediately after debarkation. Among the animals fetched from
England was a prize Durham cow, intended to mate with a
half-bred Hereford bull. Sam arranged for it to be carried in
all its pomp in a cart that local craftsmen assured him
would transport an elephant. The cow promptly fell
through the floor. It was accordingly driven on foot and
died of exhaustion halfway up the mountain. Perkes,
whose official designation was that of groom, ran a brand-
new carriage over the cliff. Baker (in his memoir)
reproduces an approximation of his letter of apology.

Honor'd Zurr,

*I'm sorry to hinform you that the carriage and osses has met
with an haccident and is tumbled down a preccipice and its a
mussy as I didn't go too. The preccipice isn't very deep being not
above heighty feet or thereabouts – the hosses is got up but is very
bad – the carriage lies on its back and we can't stir it nohow.
Mr... is very kind and has lent above a hundred niggers, but they
aint no more use than cats at liftin. Plese Zur come and see
what's to be done.*

He was drunk when the accident happened. One horse had
to be destroyed and the other died the next day. They had
been sent from Australia expressly to weather the climate.
Perkes then excelled himself. Sent down from the mountain to the accident site with an elephant, he overcame the
protests of the mahout and took him off at a fine gallop.
Refreshed by brandy and water, and finding his offers of
help declined, the groom took off again back up the pass.
In his own words, he 'tooled the old elephant along until

he came to a standstill'. Shortly afterwards, the beast keeled over and died. Perkes was, as Baker grimly observed, 'one of the few men in the world who had ridden an elephant to death'. When he finally caught up to him, the groom was being pushed round the nascent plantation in a wheelbarrow, his mate as drunk as he.

* * *

In April 2009, the Japanese pop star Hideki Kaji was beaten up by Swedes while dressed as a pineapple. Mr Kaji, 41, was shooting a music video in Malmö when he volunteered to guard the camera equipment while his crew sloped off for a break. Three muggers busted his lip, knocked loose a filling, and made off with 20,000 kronor's worth of equipment, leaving Mr Kaji unconscious and with his street-cred in tatters. Mr Kaji's hits include 'My Favourite Tofflor', 'Suddenly Sibylla' and 'Ramlösa'.

* * *

In the run-up to the 2008 Olympics in Beijing, as China prepared to turn its smiling face to the world, the entrepreneurial spirit overcame its citizens. Over the door of one restaurant, hoping to lure in hungry Westerners, was an enormous laminated sign.

On the left was the Chinese script for 'Restaurant'. Alongside it, in blue-on-green sans serif script, were the words 'Translate Server Error'.

Chinese officialdom fared little better. Beijing's Ethnic Minorities Park was crisply renamed in English: 'Racist Park'.

* * *

Sometime in the 1940s, the poet Philip Larkin was visiting his friend Bruce Montgomery, then working as a school-master in Shrewsbury. Montgomery was a beer drinker of fanatical enthusiasm, and insisted on his librarian friend matching him pint for pint.

After a tremendous session in the pub, the two went to a meeting of the school's literary society. Not long had the society been in session when Larkin – who was sitting on the chair furthest from the door, with hundreds of studious boys cross-legged on the floor between him and the exit – conceived an urgent need to relieve himself.

Larkin, a shy man, could not face the embarrassment of shuffling through the thicket of boys to the door, and dis-rupting the society. He hung on, and hung on, before the pain grew too great. This being the days of fuel rationing, Larkin was wearing thick clothes and a very heavy overcoat. Calculating, in desperation, that his clothes would serve to absorb the wee, he intentionally let go where he was sitting.

Kingsley Amis's memoirs conclude the story: 'It turned out that he had miscalculated, and under his chair there rapidly formed a pool of... Round about here, rather late on, I thought, Philip broke off telling me this story and said he wished he had never started it. He went on to extract from me some sort of promise not to go around repeating it...'

* * *

Edward de Vere, the seventeenth Earl of Oxford, is believed by some to have been the true author of the plays generally attributed to William Shakespeare. He earns his place in this book, however, as the author of the most mortifying flatulence of the Elizabethan age.

'This Earle of Oxford, making of his low obeisance to

Queen Elizabeth, happened to let a Fart,' Aubrey's *Brief Lives* tells us. 'At which he was so abashed and ashamed that he went to Travell, 7 yeeres. On his returne the Queen welcomed him home, and sayd, My Lord, I had forgott the Fart.'

* * *

The late George Brown, as Foreign Secretary, set the bar high for diplomatic gaffes. At a formal dinner in honour of the President of Turkey, he surged to his feet and declared: 'You don't want to listen to this bullshit. Let's go and have a drink.'

He frequently took his own advice. On a visit to Peru in the 1960s, he caught sight at a diplomatic function of a ravishing creature in a floor-length purple dress. He staggered over and asked for the honour of a dance.

'No,' came the reply. 'For one thing you're disgustingly drunk. For another, this is not a waltz – it is the Peruvian national anthem. And third, I am the Cardinal Archbishop of Lima.'

* * *

On an August evening in 2001, 52-year-old Dr Luis Isabel stepped into the hangar at Parafield Airport near Adelaide, Australia, intending to take his privately owned single-prop plane out for a spin. The battery, he discovered to his dismay, was flat.

So he attempted to manually start the engine by spinning the prop with his hand. The prop caught and the engine roared into life. But Dr Isabel had apparently forgotten either to put chocks under the wheels, or ensure the handbrake was engaged before he got the engine going.

His Saratoga Piper, its propeller now spinning at 2,000

rpm, began taxiing in the direction of the runway for take-off. It travelled 150 metres, its owner in hot pursuit, and its propeller sliced into perfect geometric ribbons four Piper Warriors belonging to the University of Adelaide – you can find the photographs on the Internet, and they look spectacular – before it crashed to a terminal halt in a twin-engine Seminole.

It did approximately £100,000 worth of damage. Dismissing the charges against Dr Isabel, an Adelaide magistrate described what had happened as 'a simple and reasonable mistake'.

* * *

Erratum slip from a handbook for Customs and Excise men in the Republic of Ireland: 'After contraceptives, insert fruit and vegetables.'

* * *

The Alaskan town of Nome owes its name to a mistake. Mapping the Bering Strait in the middle of the nineteenth century, a British officer wrote '?Name' by a cape whose name he didn't know. The copyist misread it as 'C. Nome' for Cape Nome, and Nome it has been ever since.

* * *

In the autumn of 1693, Samuel Pepys and his family were in their coach on their way out to Chelsea when they were overtaken by highwaymen. Three masked men descended on the coach, and put pistols to the hearts of both the coachman and Pepys himself.

The highwaymen asked what Pepys had, and he turned out his pockets. (Pepys's mistress Mary Skinner, showing more presence of mind, stuffed her bag of gold up her skirt.) He gave up £3 or so, as well as his silver ruler, his gold pencil, a set of mathematical instruments and his magnifying glass.

A look of great sadness came across Pepys's face as all this loot vanished into the highwayman's swag-bag. He made a humble plea. Would these gallant gentlemen of the road give him back just one item?

His distress worked on their hearts. The leader of the highwaymen announced with a flourish that, since Pepys was a gentleman and so, by God, was he, he would do him a favour. Why should the profession of armed robber be thought a dishonourable one? Let Pepys send to the Rummer Tavern in Charing Cross the following day, and his golden pencil would be returned to him as a gesture of courtesy.

The highwayman's name was Thomas Hoyle, and his accomplice was Samuel Gibbons. We know this from the court records. For though there may be honour among thieves, they learned the hard way that there's none among diarists.

Hoyle was apprehended by the constables the following day, just where he said he'd be, at the Rummer Tavern with Pepys's gold pencil about his person. Tough break. He and Gibbons were found guilty of felony and robbery, condemned to death, and hanged.

Pepys went about his business.

* * *

Never trust a writer, is what the experience of Pepys's highwaymen tells you. The Augustan woman of letters Lady Mary Wortley Montagu – a sometime friend of Alexander Pope –

was another case in point. To save money on her travels, she crossed the Mediterranean by wangling her way aboard a man-of-war.

On disembarking, she took the captain aside and said that she wouldn't dream of embarrassing him by trying to make him accept money for her passage. Instead, she asked that he accept a ring as a keepsake.

No, no, he said. He couldn't possibly. She insisted, and produced a gorgeous ring set with a huge emerald. Later, a friend admired the ring and asked the captain where he'd got it.

'Why, Lady Mary Wortley Montagu gave it to me,' the captain said proudly. His friend said words to the effect of 'I'd get a jeweller to have a look at that if I were you.'

He duly did. 'It was unset before him and proved a paste worth 40 shillings.'

* * *

All chefs expect to have the odd dish sent back. But a young Scotsman serving the eighteenth-century statesman Henry St John – this being the days before Gordon Ramsay and Marco Pierre White established the proper relationship between chef and customer – got more than he deserved.

St John had invited the cream of the young French nobility to supper, and instructed the unnamed chef to show off the delights of English cuisine in the form of a shoulder of mutton baked on a bed of onions.

Finding it not to his satisfaction, he leapt from the table, picked it up, and beat the maître d' over the head with it 'until he had exhausted his breath'.

'Nobly done, philosopher!' was the verdict of a fellow guest.

* * *

The philosopher William James once found himself trapped in a horse-drawn tram to Boston with a young American child who insisted on singing tunelessly and unceasingly at the top of its squeaky little voice.

The child's mother was showing not the slightest inclination to quieten the brat down. Irritated beyond endurance, he finally spoke to her: 'I think, madam, you can hardly be aware that your child's song is a cause of annoyance to the rest of us in this car.'

The woman affected to ignore him. Another passenger, however, rounded on the philosopher and said: 'How dare you, sir, address a lady in this ungentlemanly fashion?'

Now, according to James's biographer Logan Pearsall Smith, it was his then immersion in Kipling's ideas about the way violence underpinned the order of all civil societies that inspired his riposte.

'Sir,' said the philosopher, 'if you repeat that remark, I shall slap your face.'

Unfortunately, the man repeated the remark, and James was forced to slap him round the chops – at which point several of the other passengers rose in indignation and pressed their cards on the victim of the assault, promising to act as witnesses.

The tram proceeded towards Boston. James endured his mortification in a crimson-faced silence broken only by the occasional tut-tut and the high, tuneless singing of the child.

* * *

An American messenger-boy, delivering to Rudyard Kipling: 'My, Mr Kipling, it will be a great day when my folks in

Georgia hear that I actually met the man who wrote the *Rubaiyat of Omar Khayyam.*'

A similar story – told by one of my old friends as the gospel truth – concerns his encounter with a gas-station attendant in the Midwest around the end of 1997.

'Gee,' said the man with the pump in his hand, 'you're British, huh? We were all real sorry to hear about your Princess Diana. What we couldn't figure out was whut inna hell that Pavarotti was doing chasin' her in the first place...'

* * *

On his deathbed, Bruce Chatwin gave his friend Jonathan Hope a knife used in Aboriginal initiation ceremonies that he had found in the bush. 'It's obviously made from some sort of desert opal,' he said. 'It's a wonderful colour, almost the colour of chartreuse.'

Not long afterwards, Hope showed it to the Director of the Australian National Gallery. 'Hmm,' he said, 'amazing what the Abos can do with a bit of an old beer bottle.'

THE COURSE OF TRUE LOVE

<T-Wolf>: man, my girlfriend left me for some faggot named robert
<RdAwG20>: you don't live in Hope mills do you?
<T-Wolf>: ya, why man?
<RdAwG20>: lol, just wondering, was her namne alisson?
<T-Wolf>: you mother fucker

(Fragment from an Internet chat room,
archived at www.bash.org)

* * *

In 1978, Vera Czernak of Prague discovered that her husband had been cheating on her. Distraught, she threw herself out of their third-storey window. She landed on her husband, who was killed. Mrs Czernak was taken to hospital and made a full recovery.

* * *

'Dear Christ! the very prison walls/ Suddenly seemed to reel,/ And the sky above my head became/ Like a casque of scorching steel...' There's plenty of that sort of nonsense in Oscar Wilde's poem *The Ballad of Reading Gaol*. But let's not forget: the switch-hitting Anglo-Irish genius had only himself to blame.

The reason Wilde ended up in chokey was not that a brutal and intolerant society refused to countenance his sensitive crimes – or at least, not entirely. It was that he picked a fight he could not win.

The problem was, as so often, the disapproval of the prospective in-laws. The Marquess of Queensberry had been on Wilde's case ever since he discovered that Wilde was dating his son, Lord Alfred Douglas.

He confronted Wilde at home, and was shown the door. He booked tickets for the opening night of *The Importance of Being Earnest*. There, he planned to bombard the eminent aesthete, who preferred green carnations, with turnips. He was thwarted. Finally, he left a calling card for 'Oscar Wilde posing as a somdomite'.

Actually, his handwriting is hard to make out. It could have been 'posing somdomite'. And it could have been, as the porter at the hotel thought, 'ponce and sodomite'. Whichever way you read it, though, this winning combination of bigotry and illiteracy did not intend to extend the hand of friendship.

But these were bird-bolts Wilde took for cannonballs. Instead of ignoring him, Wilde sued him for criminal libel. A hard case to sustain – unless you argued that it was libellous to accuse him of 'posing as a somdomite' when he was, patently, the real thing. Or that he wasn't a 'ponce and somdomite' since – unless you disapproved very strongly of his plays – you couldn't accuse him of living off immoral earnings. Neither of these ingenious but, frankly, tracing-paper-thin arguments was attempted.

In the course of the libel trial, the Marquess's lawyers dug up and publicized as much evidence of Wilde's life in London's gay and criminal demi-monde as they could find. And the collapse of the libel trial set in train criminal proceedings against him for gross indecency.

Each man, as a wise fellow wrote, kills the thing he loves.

* * *

'There is no art form which attempts the sublime while defying the ridiculous with quite the foolhardiness of opera,' wrote the late Peter Ustinov. Sometimes, though, the direction of travel is opposite. Take, for instance, the stagehands in a 1960 production of *Tosca* in New York, who, after suffering through weeks of rehearsals with a more than usually high-maintenance soprano, set about defying the sublime by attempting the ridiculous.

The story of *Tosca* ends with the hefty warbler in the title role considerably bent out of shape. She thought her boyfriend was about to be the victim of a fake execution, but then it turns out to have been a real execution. He's not playing dead: he's actually dead. Boo hoo! Trilling tragically, she mounts the battlements of the castle and throws herself off, while the orchestra blares her tragic death theme.

On this occasion, things did not go as planned. 'O Scarpia, avanti a Dio!' she sobbed, and hurled herself off the battlements. Then – BOINGGGG!!! – she bounced right back into sight with her skirts around her ears and an expression of astonishment on her face.

For the mattress that should have been there to break the soprano's fall, the stagehands had substituted a trampoline.

Tosca vanished below the battlements and then – BOINGGGG!! – reappeared for a second time, this time upside-down and screaming with rage.

She reached the peak of her trajectory and again descended below the ramparts.

BOINNGGG!

There she was again, now giggling maniacally. She never again sang Tosca.

That soprano, mind you, is not the only victim the ramparts of Castel Sant'Angelo have claimed over the years.

In a 1961 production in San Francisco, the director was relying on a badly under-rehearsed firing squad. A ragged crew of students recruited from the campus of a local college, they hadn't the first idea how the plot of the opera proceeded.

'What do we do?' they pestered the director. 'When do we come on? When do we leave?' A scheduling foul-up meant that the dress rehearsal was cancelled.

'Exit with the principals!' he hissed as they trooped on stage from the wings. First, they managed to shoot the wrong person. Then, as the opera reached its climax and they found themselves on stage with Tosca alone, they watched her jump over the battlements and vanish.

'Exit with the principals,' they thought. And so, dutifully, the whole firing squad trooped up to the castle walls and, like operatic lemmings, threw themselves off en masse.

* * *

On a sultry afternoon in 1999, 23-year-old Jose Noh borrowed the hearse from work, drove it into a Mexico City warehouse, and sneaked his sweetheart into the back to make love. Afterwards they drifted off in each other's arms.

They were later found dead in the back of the coffin-wagon, in a warehouse filled with carbon monoxide. Jose had left the motor running so they could keep the air-conditioning on.

* * *

The pioneering feminist Mary Wollstonecraft – mother of Mary Shelley and author of *A Vindication of the Rights of Women* – took glum one day and resolved to kill herself. She'd been over to Paris to enjoy the Revolution, had a fling with an American called Gilbert Imlay, and then having been deserted by him and left holding the baby decided suicide was the only way forward.

She wrote Gilbert a note, announcing her intentions, and set off on foot to throw herself from Battersea Bridge. When she got there, she decided there were too many people about. She was shy.

Already slightly soggy from the incessant drizzle, she persuaded a boatman to hire her his boat, and paddled it off downriver towards Putney. She beached it under Putney Bridge, and climbed aloft. The road onto the bridge was barred at both ends by a tollgate, so she fished inside her wet togs and paid her halfpenny toll, then made her way to the middle of the bridge, hauled herself over the railings, and jumped.

Rather than cease upon the midnight with no pain, she hit the water with a splash, and her skirts bobbed up around her ears, keeping her afloat. Some watermen saw her fall, fished her out, and took her to 'a none too respectable' pub to dry off.

She resigned herself to live.

* * *

Sir William Davenant, a Poet Laureate of the seventeenth century, had no small opinion of his own talents. He fancied that he wrote with the very spirit of Shakespeare – and, indeed, rather pleased by the idea that some people might believe he was the bard's son, used to offer this as a theory 'when he was pleasant over a glass of wine'.

He boasted to his intimate friends, among them Samuel Butler, that during his annual journey to Warwickshire, Shakespeare had been in the habit of stopping off overnight at this very house in Oxfordshire, and had been – we're all men of the world, need I spell it out? – 'exceedingly respected' there.

Naturally, the story got back to the one person who might not regard it as a source of pride. 'He would tell them the story as above,' reports Aubrey cheerfully, 'in which way his mother had a very light report, whereby she was called a whore.'

* * *

D. H. Lawrence's wife, Frieda, told Harold Nicolson that Lawrence had once told her: 'Frieda, if people really knew what you were like, they would strangle you.'

Nicolson, startled, asked her: 'Did he say that angrily?'

'No – very quietly,' Mrs Lawrence replied, adding: 'after several minutes' deep thought.'

* * *

Frederick Delius's opera *A Village Romeo and Juliet* reaches its unusual emotional climax when the lovers – trysting in a boat on the lake – scuttle it and go to a watery grave together.

In a 1920 London production, however, the conductor's inept assistant cued the stagehands to sink the boat four pages early. The lovers sang their last duet from the bottom of the lake.

The following day's performance corrected the error, in the process inadvertently giving the opera a happy ending.

The assistant forgot to cue the stagehands altogether, the boat didn't sink and the lovers didn't drown.

* * *

'T. S. Eliot writes books for me... King Farouk's on tenter-hooks for me,' sung Eartha Kitt in her 1952 hit 'Monotonous'. Among her other improbable claims were that 'Harry S. Truman plays bop for me' and that Chiang Kai-shek sent her cups of tea.

T. S. Eliot – a great lover of musical theatre, as any student of *The Waste Land* knows – was delighted at his inclusion in the song, and immediately sent Kitt a bunch of roses with a complimentary card. She never replied, but Eliot learned that the roses had arrived when a sceptical newspaper reported: 'Eartha Kitt claims that T. S. Eliot sent her a bouquet'.

* * *

The Jewish-Hungarian writer Arthur Koestler was a ladies' man but not, it should be said, much of a charmer. He feuded with a male acquaintance on discovering that the man had warned a certain girl he had his eye on that Koestler wore a hairnet in bed. It was quite untrue, he insisted. 'Like every civilized Continental,' he sniffed, he only wore his hairnet in the bath.

SOD'S WAR

In 1947, the battle-class destroyer *HMS Saintes* was selected to trial a new gun, the 4.5-inch twin turret, which was to become the standard main armament for the British navy's destroyer fleet.

The tug *HMS Buccaneer* towed a target across *Saintes*'s bows to test the accuracy of the guns. *Saintes* fired, missed the target, and sank *HMS Buccaneer*.

* * *

In 1981, a small shipbuilding company in Ameglia, Italy, was awarded the contract that they thought would make their name on the international scene. The Malaysian government wanted Intermarine to build – at a cost of £4 million – a minesweeper and three military launches; bigger ships by far than anything the company had built before.

The project took two years, coming in on time and within the budget. Unfortunately, it was only then that they realized that across the waterway that connected their shipyard on the Magra River with the Mediterranean was the Colombiera Bridge – which was too low for any of the new ships to pass under. Intermarine volunteered to pay the entire cost of dismantling and rebuilding the bridge, but the town council refused permission. The Malaysian navy went without its ships; and Intermarine has yet to present a serious threat to Cunard.

* * *

During the Second World War, considerable energy and ingenuity was expended by the camoufleurs, who contrived for the defence of the realm to disguise munitions factories as hills, machine-gun nests as circus tents, and tanks as garden sheds.

One major project concerned a fake munitions factory – designed to fool German bombers into bombarding it rather than the real thing – constructed near Dover of wood and canvas by a deputation of artists from the Slade. Just as the last lick of paint had been applied to the structure and the artists were retiring to toast their handiwork, a German bomber came out of the evening sun and descended on the fake factory. It waggled its wings, the bomb bay doors opened, and right into the middle of the target it dropped a beautifully manufactured balsa wood bomb.

* * *

In one of his letters, Evelyn Waugh tells the story of the ill-fated attempt by the lads of No.3 Commando to ingratiate themselves with Lord Glasgow. Knowing that he had on his land an old tree stump he wanted rid of; they offered to blow it up for him.

He very gratefully accepted their offer – once reassured that their sappers could fell a tree on a sixpence and that the plantation of young trees nearby on which he doted would come to no harm – and by way of thanks invited them round to lunch on the day of the explosion.

As the hour approached, Col. Durnford-Slater took his subaltern aside and asked whether he'd put enough explosive in the tree. He was told that there was exactly 75lb of dynamite in the stump – the chap had mathematically calculated the amount necessary to flatten the stump without disturbing the surrounding trees.

'Best add a smidgeon more,' he commanded the subaltern, by now feeling the pleasurable effects of his host's port, 'just to make sure'. His orders were duly obeyed.

'Watch this,' Col. Durnford-Slater advised Lord Glasgow, with no small self-satisfaction, when the appointed hour of the explosion came. The fuse was lit. Far from falling neatly at the appointed angle, the tree-stump – along with half an acre of soil and the entire plantation of saplings on which Lord Glasgow doted – was blown fifty feet into the air.

'Sir, I made a mistake,' the subaltern confessed to his Colonel as the lunch party dodged the falling debris. 'It should have been 7.5lb, not 75lb.' Puce with mortification, Lord Glasgow stalked back up the drive in silence – only to round the corner and see that the explosion had shattered every pane of glass in the castle.

With a sob, Lord Glasgow ran to the lavatory to hide his grief. Where, when he pulled the chain, the ceiling collapsed on him.

* * *

If you were a German soldier in Normandy after D-Day, you can be regarded as already having fallen victim, more or less, to Sod's Law. Those whose paths crossed that of Private Smith of the 79th Infantry Division, however, were even unluckier than most.

As Antony Beevor's *D-Day* records, Private Smith was

among troops fighting in the Cotentin Peninsula when, emboldened by a certain amount of Calvados, he took a German fort single-handedly.

Noticing the door of the fort ajar, Smith – who was armed with only a .45 pistol – staggered inside and shot dead the soldiers standing around the entrance. Then Smith – 'who was in truth,' as the official report noted, 'stewed to the ears' – went from room to room 'shooting and shouting, and as he appeared at each door, the Germans inside, thinking the whole American army was in the fort, gave up'.

Smith marched his prisoners out into the open, handed them over to his battalion, and then returned to the fort, stumbling into a room filled with wounded Germans. 'Declaring to all and sundry that the only good German was a dead one, Smith made good Germans out of several of them before he could be stopped.'

* * *

John Sedgwick was one of the more accident-prone of the Union's senior commanders in the American Civil War. His first engagement was, from the point of view of his safety, a complete success. He missed the first action of the Civil War because of a runny tummy.

Back on fighting form for the battle of Glendale, he was wounded in the arm and leg. He was promoted. Ordered to lead a division of 5,400 men into the Battle of Antietam – with reconnaissance that, with the benefit of hindsight, hadn't been of the finest – he ended up after a morning's fighting back where he started less 2,200 casualties, and having been shot in the arm (again), leg (again) and shoulder.

His injuries prevented him getting involved in the Battle of Fredericksburg, and he showed up late for the Battle of Gettysburg – in time to catch the speeches but not to get much involved in the fighting. Again, from the point of view of his safety, this was a complete success.

Major General Sedgwick, as he was by then, turned up on time for the Battle of Spotsylvania Court House, in May 1864. At the outset of the action, he was directing artillery ahead of the left flank of the Confederate troops. He noticed that his men were ducking for cover because Confederate sharpshooters were shooting at them.

Striding into open ground, he urged them to take courage.

'What? Men dodging this way for single bullets?' he chided them. 'What will you do when they open fire along the whole line? I am ashamed of you. They couldn't hit an elephant at this distance.'

He repeated, 'I'm ashamed of you, dodging that way. They couldn't hit an elephant at this dist...'

He was at that instant felled by a bullet below his left eye.

* * *

Few set battles in military history have been quite such unqualified disasters as the Battle of Tanga – the encounter that kicked off the Great War in Africa and set the tone for much of the rest of it.

The first news of the outbreak of hostilities in Europe was conveyed to the British district commissioner in Northern Nyasaland in the coded message 'Tipsified Pumgirdles Germany Novel', and the war got no less inane from then on in.

In November 1914, Britain's Indian Expeditionary Force moved to mount an amphibious attack on the seaport of

Tanga – the foothold by which they intended to sweep in and capture German East Africa.

Being good chaps, they told the Germans roughly what they were proposing to do. There having been a previous understanding that the port would be allowed to remain neutral, the Brits decided it was only fair to send an advance guard – in the form of the cruiser *HMS Fox* – to tell Johnny Kraut that all bets were off. The commander of the port was given one hour to lower the German flag. He didn't. *HMS Fox* waddled off to call up the landing force.

This should have been a doddle. Tanga remained, near as dammit, undefended. The harbour was not mined. The Germans – even after having taken the chance to reinforce the port afforded by the Brits spending a day and a half sweeping for non-existent mines – were poorly equipped, and outnumbered eight to one.

On the other hand, the Indian Expeditionary Force had spent weeks at sea – boiling hot and foully provisioned – and were all sick as dogs. Their commander had ignored suggestions to put them ashore in Mombasa to get them back up to strength before the attack.

They put in without proper reconnaissance of what was ahead, and worried that Johnny Hun might be planning something, they played it safe by setting down a mile away, out of sight of the port. Their landing area turned out to be a godforsaken mangrove swamp lifting with tsetse flies, leeches and water-snakes.

Their eventual advance on the port was thwarted by their not being able to see anything through the cocoa plantations that surrounded it. When a couple of British officers climbed a hill to get a better look, they were shot dead. So jumpy were the wretched Indian troops that when one of their own rifles went off by accident, a hundred of them fled into the sea.

Another brigade found themselves marching, dizzy with heatstroke, through a field of eight-foot-tall corn – surrounded by trees from which enemy snipers shot at the tops of their heads.

They were in short order bogged down in the jungle, mired in the built-up areas of the port, and routed by a cunning and noisy German ambush (headed by the Prussian tactical genius Paul von Lettow-Vorbeck, presently known as 'von Lettow-Fallback' for his mastery of asymmetric warfare).

As the Expeditionary Force retreated, they disturbed a number of bees' nests, which swarmed indiscriminately on troops of both sides, stinging some men more than a hundred times. Then the Germans, thanks to a series of errors in communication, also retreated. Had the IEF known of this, they could have turned round and won the day. But they didn't, because their reconnaissance was lousy and they were too busy trying to find the Wasp-Eze.

Instead, a general retreat was ordered, and the British forces put back out to sea having taken 847 casualties. Their attack had donated the enemy enough rifles to arm three whole companies of native fighters, sixteen machine guns, a handful of field telephones, enough clothing to last the German Schutztruppe through the whole of the following year, and 600,000 rounds of ammunition.

* * *

In 1944, as General 'Blood and Guts' Patton's Third Army was rolling back the Nazis in France, one war correspondent went out of his way to beat his rivals to the punch. Determined to be the first on the scene to witness the liberation of Chartres, he turned up a full two days before the

Allied forces – and was promptly taken prisoner by the Germans.

* * *

It was 6 August. Tsutomu Yamaguchi, a Japanese engineer who worked designing oil tankers for Mitsubishi, rose early. He had spent three months working at his firm's shipyard 180 miles from home, and was looking forward to getting back to see his family. He and two colleagues collected their belongings and set out from their lodgings to catch the train west.

As they went, though, he remembered he had left something in the office, so waved them off and set off to retrieve it. He remembers hearing the buzz of an aeroplane's engines circling overhead, just after 8.15 a.m. He thought nothing of it.

The year was 1945, the city Mr Yamaguchi had been working in was Hiroshima – and the aeroplane circling overhead was the *Enola Gay*.

Mr Yamaguchi was less than two miles from ground zero when 'Little Boy' exploded in the air 1,900 feet up. There was a blinding flash of light and a deafening bang. Mr Yamaguchi was knocked off his feet by the force of the blast, and his skin burnt. He had no idea what had just happened. Somehow, he found his way to an air-raid shelter, where he spent the night.

The following day, he stumbled through the wreckage of Hiroshima, swaddled in bandages, to get the train back to his home town.

Trouper that he was, and still badly burned, Mr Yamaguchi nevertheless reported for work the following morning.

On the morning of his second day back at work in his home town, he was just in the middle of telling his boss what had happened in Hiroshima (his boss was incredulous, he said, at the idea that a single bomb could destroy an entire city) when once again there was a blinding flash of light, a deafening bang, and Mr Yamaguchi was knocked flat by a burning blast of heat.

His home town was, of course, Nagasaki – and Mr Yamaguchi was once again at ground zero.

Some 140,000 civilians are estimated to have died as a result of America's attack on Hiroshima – either instantly, or from the after-effects of radiation. The death toll in Nagasaki was 70,000.

Mr Yamaguchi, interviewed in March 2009 at the age of 93, reported that he was in good health but 'a little deaf in one ear'.

* * *

In 1978, a diver accidentally left a paint-scraper in the torpedo tube of the US nuclear submarine *Swordfish*. The paint-scraper, worth less than a pound, jammed the torpedo loading system. In order to remove it, the submarine had to be brought onto dry land. The repairs cost a reported £84,000.

* * *

'Half a league, half a league,/ Half a league onward/ All in the valley of Death/ Rode the six-hundred.' So did Alfred, Lord Tennyson commemorate the epic balls-up that was the Charge of the Light Brigade at the Battle of Balaclava.

The root of the problem seems to have been a somewhat ambiguous order: 'Lord Raglan wishes the cavalry to advance rapidly to the front – follow the enemy and try to prevent the enemy carrying away the guns. Troop Horse Artillery may accompany. French cavalry is on your left. R. Airey. Immediate.'

Had communications been more efficient in those days, 'NOT **THOSE** GUNS!' is what, many historians agree, the follow-up order would have read. It's widely thought that what Lord Raglan might have meant was for the Light Brigade to secure a handful of Turkish guns from some redoubts that had been captured on the other side of the hill.

But the order passed from Lord Raglan to Brigadier Airey, to Captain Nolan, to Lord Lucan (a previous one) and down, finally, to the Light Brigade's commander, Lord Cardigan. And off they charged. The 673 plucky horsemen of this cavalry brigade headed down a narrow valley with fifty Cossack guns and twenty battalions of infantry at the other end of it.

'NOT **THOSE** GUNS!' may, in fact, have been exactly the message that Captain Nolan – who had handed down the original orders – was intending to convey when he galloped out across the front of his troops waving his sword wildly in the air. We'll never know, because he was blown up almost immediately by a Russian artillery shell.

Nolan's attempt to head off the charge, Cardigan later said, had enraged him. He thought he was trying to take over the leadership and steal his thunder. Cardigan put his head down and didn't look back.

So it was towards those guns, and between those guns, that the Light Brigade was now committed to charging. And charge they did. And blown to bits they were.

As Lord Cardigan later recalled, the situation was distinctly sub-optimal, from the charging point of view:

> We advanced down a gradual descent of more than three-
> quarters of a mile, with the batteries vomiting forth upon
> us shells and shot, round and grape, with one battery on

our right flank and another on the left, and all the interme-
diate ground covered with the Russian riflemen; so that
when we came to within a distance of fifty yards from the
mouths of the artillery which had been hurling destruction
upon us, we were, in fact, surrounded and encircled by a
blaze of fire, in addition to the fire of the riflemen upon
our flanks.

Who, precisely, was to blame? The answer is outwith the
scope of the present study.

A summary of the event on the National Archives website captures it nicely, though: 'Raglan's order was imprecise,
Airey's drafting of the order was ambiguous, Nolan failed to
explain the order to Lucan adequately, Lucan failed to question Nolan properly to establish his commander's intent and
Cardigan failed to seek adequate clarification from Lucan.'

* * *

It was 10 August 1628. There was a gentle breeze blowing
from the southwest, and the day was a fair one. Sweden –
once a piddling little Scandinavian kingdom – was crescent
as a player on the international stage and just enjoying the
full flowering of its *Stormaktstiden*, or 'Age of Greatness', a
decade into the reign of its go-ahead ruler, King Gustavus
Adolphus.

This was a special day in Swedish history. The mighty warship *Vasa* – pride of the Swedish fleet and incarnation of the
kingdom's imperial ambitions – sailed out on her maiden
voyage from the Skeppsgården shipyard in Stockholm.
Gathered at the waterside were thousands of ordinary
Swedes, agog at this miracle of naval engineering.

Around her hull were arrayed five hundred brightly

painted sculptures of mermaids, sea-monsters, Tritons, and other figures of classical heroism. High on the transom was a sculpture of the great Gustavus Adolphus as a young boy with flowing blond hair, and the figurehead of the boat was a ten-foot-long lion. The most expensive pigments available had been used to paint the sculptures, and the body of the boat was painted bright red – where it was not gaudy with gold leaf.

Vasa was the most powerful warship in the world. She carried forty-eight heavy guns, six howitzers, and could send nearly six hundred pounds of ammo sailing towards the enemy from a single broadside. She took two years to build.

On the day of her maiden voyage, she was headed to the naval station at Älvsnabben, whence she was to join the Baltic fleet in the Thirty Years' War. The ship was towed to the south of the harbour, three of her ten sails were set, and the gun ports opened in anticipation of a thunderous salute as she left harbour.

The problem was, all those guns made the old girl a bit top-heavy. Most ships with a comparable broadside – there weren't any at the time, but a century or so later they were plentiful – needed to be much deeper in the keel and much broader in the beam. The shipbuilders were able to calculate this, but the glorious and mighty warrior-king Gustavus Augustus didn't get to be a glorious and mighty warrior-king without being a shade tetchy – so they slightly chickened out of mentioning it.

As she left the lee of the port, the breeze picked up a bit and she tipped over on her side. We can only imagine the gasps from the crowd. She righted herself – then a second gust of wind finished her off. Water flooded in through the gun ports, and – having travelled only 400 feet from shore – she went promptly to the bottom.

* * *

In 1975, the Peruvian Air Force mounted a show of strength to celebrate Air Force Week. Fourteen beaten-up fishing boats were cast adrift at sea, overflown and bombarded by a detachment of thirty jet fighters. More than a hundred bombs were dropped, and the ships were strafed with guns.

When the smoke cleared, all fourteen boats were still merrily afloat. On landing, two of the fighters taxied into each other on the runway and were written off.

* * *

Britain's answer to the German U-Boat were the K-Class submarines – 100-metre-long steam-powered submersibles that cost £340,000 a pop, and could do 24 knots on the surface. Minor design faults aside – travelling at speed on the surface could cause the front of the boat to plunge under-water, and big waves tended to pour down the funnels and put the boilers out – they were the pride of the fleet.

They saw heroic action in the First World War, and our seafaring nation is able to boast that not one was ever lost through enemy action. Six of the eighteen built, however, sank by accident.

K1 crashed into K4 off the coast of Denmark and had to be scuttled.

K2 caught fire on her maiden dive. In 1924, she collided with K12 as they were leaving Portland Harbour.

K3 plunged nose-first to the bottom in December 1916 (giving a thrill of patriotic pride, no doubt, to the future King George VI, who happened to be on board at the time), got stuck in mud and took twenty minutes to free. The following

January her boiler room flooded in the North Sea. The year after that she again dived unexpectedly and crashed into the seabed, causing massive damage to her hull.

K4, having survived the collision that did for K1, was less lucky in the sarcastically named 'Battle of May Island', the debacle that outright did for two of the K-Class submarines, seriously damaged four more of them, as well as badly dinging a couple of battlecruisers.

It was the last night of January, 1918, when a flotilla of around forty vessels passed through the mouth of the Firth of Forth en route to exercises in Scapa Flow. The trouble started when the flotilla attempted to change course for the north.

K22 crashed into K14. Then the battlecruiser *Inflexible* crashed into K22 (*Inflexible* lived up to her name, but K22 bent round at right angles and sank till only the conning tower could be seen above the surface of the water).

Fearless crashed into K17, which went straight to the bottom. Then, as the submarines behind took lumbering evasive action, things got worse. While attempting to avoid colliding with K3, K4 was nearly cut in half by K6 and then rammed by K7 before heading, too, with grim inevitability for the seabed.

K5 was not involved in the Battle of May Island. She went down with all hands for no apparent reason during exercises in the Bay of Biscay.

K10 foundered while being towed in 1922.

K13 sank during sea-trials in a Scottish loch when her hatches failed to shut properly on diving. Salvaged and recommissioned as K22, she would go on to take a distinguished role in the Battle of May Island.

K15 – anxious to cut to the chase – spontaneously sank at her mooring in Portsmouth Harbour in 1921.

Only one K-boat ever engaged the enemy. It hit a U-boat amidships with a torpedo. The torpedo failed to explode.

* * *

In September 1980, an engineer conducting routine maintenance at an Arkansas ICBM silo dropped a wrench. The wrench bounced off a missile and punctured its pressurized fuel tank. The silo had to be evacuated. Eight hours later an explosion blew the 740-ton steel-and-concrete door clean off, and hurled a nuclear warhead 600 feet into the air.

* * *

The ancient city of Amykles sat by the Eurotas River, just southwest of Sparta. The Spartans – as Zack Snyder's thrillingly homoerotic film *300* confirms – were a bit of a stabby bunch, and their Amyklean neighbours spent a demoralizing amount of time speculating that they'd be next in line for a good stabbing, burning and pillaging from the Spartans.

Finally, the city authorities passed a decree forbidding anyone from even mentioning Spartans, stabbing, or anything else liable to spread alarm and despondency. Not long afterwards, the Spartans did indeed mount an invasion. Because none of those who saw them coming dared mention it, the town was taken entirely by surprise and overrun.

The ancient city is now a ruin, and modern Amykles, next door, is a wee village with no more than five hundred people living there. All of them, I fancy, talk incessantly of Spartans.

OUT FOR A DUCK

For the citizens of Lindsay, Ontario, 1958 was a proud year. The Lindsay Chamber of Commerce had approved a $12,500 grant, in the interests of 'cultural enrichment', to make the town the host of the very first bullfight in Canada's history.

The eyes of the world were upon the little town on the Scugog River, as, on the evening of 21 July, four of Mexico's finest matadors – at their head the dashing 26-year-old Rudolpho Rodriguez – arrived to star in the festivities.

Their triumphal arrival was not as they might have hoped. Mr Rodriguez and his fellow matadors were greeted by a solitary member of the Lindsay Chamber of Commerce, the others being at the time mired in a town council meeting over whether to approve a proposal to decorate the town in honour of the bullfighters. The proposal was rejected.

Meanwhile the six fighting bulls – also being imported from Mexico for the event – had been turned back at the Texas border for quarantine reasons, and didn't arrive until three weeks later. By this time, Mr Rodriguez had gone home.

Being pacific and Canadian by nature, the Chamber of Commerce had decided that the bullfight would be 'bloodless'; yet this still was not enough to allay the zealots of the Ontario Society for the Prevention of Cruelty to Animals. They vowed to 'do everything in our power to prevent "bloodless bullfighting" in Lindsay'.

Nevertheless, the event pressed ahead – and on 22 and 23 August, only three weeks late and one matador short, Lindsay staged a bullfight in which no bulls were fought.

It was adjudged a great success, and no other bullfights have ever been held in Canada.

* * *

The roguish Edwardian MP Horatio Bottomley – described in the late William Donaldson's invaluable reference *Rogues, Villains and Eccentrics* as 'the most remarkable swindler of his, or any other, time' – hit on a sure-fire scheme for self-enrichment.

He bought, according to that pioneering historian of catastrophe, Stephen Pile, all six of the nags that were to run in a horse-race at the coastal town of Blankenberghe in Belgium. He hired six jockeys to ride them, and gave these men very firm instructions as to which order the horses should finish the race in. Then he filled his boots at the bookies.

Halfway through the race, an impenetrably thick mist blew in from the sea and it became impossible for rider to see track, horse to see horse, and anyone to see the finishing line. The race ended in utter chaos and Bottomley lost his stack.

You can't keep a good man down, however. Bottomley invariably recovered from bankruptcy by inventing a fresh way of swindling innocent people out of their money. Typical of the man's endeavours was the Anglo-Austrian Union, which invited investors to buy shares in various enterprises in Austria. It never bought anything. At the end of its first year's trading, its accountants reported receipts of £93,000, against expenditures ('Cash To Mr Bottomley') of £88,500. Its balance at the bank was £26: 'insufficient funds to pay the expense of printing this report'. That was probably for the best.

When his various crooked schemes finally caught up with him, he was sentenced to seven years in prison. A visitor to the prison who came upon the former Liberal MP stitching mailbags is said to have greeted him with the words: 'Sewing, Bottomley?'

'No,' he replied lugubriously. 'Reaping.'

* * *

In 1938, after completing a transcontinental flight from Long Beach, California, to New York, the dashing American aviator Douglas Corrigan set out on the return journey. He steered his little plane into the air from Floyd Bennet airfield in Brooklyn before, to the bemusement of those on the ground, appearing to head off in an easterly direction.

A bit over twenty-eight hours later, Corrigan touched down in Dublin having flown across the Atlantic by mistake.

He made the journey in a tiny monoplane he couldn't see out the front of. He had no radio, his compass was twenty years old, and he was provisioned with only two chocolate bars and a couple of boxes of figs.

A journalist who saw his plane in Dublin described it as being 'like a boy would build a scooter out of a soapbox and a pair of old roller skates'. 'The nose of the engine hood was a mass of patches soldered by Corrigan himself into a crazy-quilt design. The door behind which Corrigan crouched for twenty-eight hours was fastened together with a piece of baling wire.'

It took a six-hundred-word telegram just to list all the rules Corrigan had been in violation of. His pilot's licence was suspended and he and his plane had to return to New York by ship.

The world, however, went wild for him. A front page headline on the *New York Post* proclaimed, in mirror writing, 'Hail Wrong Way Corrigan', and he returned to a ticker-tape parade down Broadway, attended by more people than had turned out to fete Lindbergh for flying across the Atlantic deliberately.

Corrigan said afterwards: 'I want to do this trip again.'

* * *

Ever since the dawn of the anagram, the forces of embuggerance have been ranged against the anagrammer. Anagrams generated at random, in particular, tend to cause embarrassment in direct proportion to how publicly they are displayed.

This rule goes double for Hasbro, the second largest toy manufacturer in the world, and the company that owns Scrabble.

In January 2008, a 'Scrabblegram' puzzle in the *Washington Post* invited readers to rearrange the letters E,U,T,T,S,X and B to make a seven-letter word. The answer they were looking for was 'SUBTEXT' – which makes it all the sweeter that the answer most readers came up with was 'BUTTSEX'. The Scrabblegram directly below assured readers: 'KATYDID'. (That's the name of a sort of insect.)

In February 2009, the random word generator placed as 'Scrabble Word of the Day' on Hasbro's website the word 'DILDO', earnestly glossed as 'an object used as a penis substitute'. This was later amended to 'TRIPLY'. If you get 'DILDO' on a triple, it scores 21 points in Scrabble.

The influence of Sod's workings on Scrabble are well attested in the Scrabble-playing community. A website devoted to people sharing photographs of impossible Scrabble hands has received more than 150,000 visitors.

* * *

Shridhar Chillal of Pune, India, began growing his nails after being challenged to a nail-growing competition by one of his teachers. Forty-five years later the nails on his left hand totalled more than six metres in length, he had been included in the *Guinness Book of Records*, and the bet with his teacher was won.

Mr Chillal's competitive determination did have unlooked-for side-effects. His job as a photographer's assistant was next to impossible to do one-handed. He had a twenty-four-hour headache, painful and permanently disfigured fingers, was deaf in his left ear and, as he complained ungallantly to reporters: 'It took me seven years to get married, because no girl wanted anything to do with these nails. Eventually I married a close relative with a hare lip.'

He added: 'Typing is out of the question.'

* * *

In 1970, two natives of Haruku, Indonesia – Messrs Djambi and Hasnuddin – fell into dispute over the ownership of a sage tree that bordered their properties. They decided to resolve the dispute by seeing who could hold his breath underwater the longest. They both weighted themselves with stones, walked into the sea and drowned.

The sage tree survived for several years.

* * *

Sunrise on a hazy and windless morning outside North Battlefield, Saskatchewan. It was 27 May 2008, and the French daredevil Michel Fournier was about to realize the dream of a lifetime.

Rising above the Saskatchewan plains, the still-rosy sun gilding its silver flanks, was a magnificent sight. A 90-metre-tall hi-tech balloon, made of a polyethylene film only 16 microns thick – and all but filled, now, with the 4,000 cubic metres of helium required for take-off.

The project – after two previous disappointments – was at last on track. He had been waiting twenty years, and had spent more than $12 million, for this moment. The balloon, described by one observer as a 'giant silver squid', would take M. Fournier to the very edge of space – whence he would launch 'Le Grand Saut'.

He would skydive from 40 kilometres above the surface of the earth: higher than any human being had ever skydived. He was to spend fifteen minutes in free-fall, crashing through the sound barrier and reaching speeds of 1,600 kph. His parachute would open less than 7 kilometres from the ground.

The balloon wobbled into the air, filled steadily with helium, and at last – lift-off! 'Oooh!' said the crowd as it slipped the surly bonds of earth. 'Aah!' they marvelled as a siren honked from the base of the balloon. 'Awww...' they sighed, as it became clear that the balloon – soon to be thousands of metres above them, as planned – was not attached to M. Fournier.

* * *

In 1991, an Iranian hunter near Teheran pinned a snake to the ground with the butt of his rifle. The snake slid its tail through the trigger guard and discharged the gun, killing the man instantly.

* * *

In February 2009, the world-class skier Lindsay Vonn won two gold medals in the World Championships. At a party to celebrate, she severed a tendon and opened her thumb up to the bone trying to open a champagne bottle to celebrate her win. She missed her next race and fell over in her final one because she couldn't hold her ski-pole properly.

* * *

The career of the daredevil stunt motorcyclist Evel Knievel is one of the twentieth century's greatest instances of one man's determination to break as many bones as possible triumphing over the occasional unforeseen instance of good luck.

He got off to an inauspicious start, leaping to polite applause over a box of rattlesnakes and a couple of mountain lions without so much as dislocating a thumb. Fans had to wait until the third live performance, in 1966, of *Evel Knievel and his Motorcycle Daredevils*, before they got a sense of what he was capable of.

Evel announced his intention to jump spreadeagle over a speeding motorcycle. He mistimed his jump, the Motorcycle Daredevil hit him smack in the groin, and Evel was hurled 15 feet into the air by his balls.

We can only imagine.

When Evel emerged from hospital, he decided to up the ante, and started jumping cars. By June, he was back to form, sailing over twelve parked cars and most of a panel truck – before ploughing into the landing ramp, smashing his arm and several ribs.

When Evel emerged from hospital, he decided to up the ante again. So the following May, he jumped sixteen parked cars. To the crowd's by now acute disappointment, he landed safely. So he tried it again two months later. Result! He smashed his left wrist, right knee, and two ribs.

When Evel emerged from hospital, he decided to up the

ante again. So he persuaded the management of the Caesar's Palace casino in Las Vegas to let him try to jump their enormous fountains at the end of December.

On the day of the jump, Evel swaggered through the casino, dropped a hundred bucks on blackjack, threw back a shot of bourbon, and – flanked by gorgeous showgirls – emerged to face his public. To triumphal music, he roared up the jump ramp, sailed into the air, came up short and went flying over the handlebars. This time he managed to smash his pelvis and femur, fracture both ankles, a hip and a wrist. He spent twenty-nine days in a coma.

Now he was really hitting his stride. Before every jump, he would mutter to himself: 'God, take care of me. Here I come...' We can only conclude that God was in a whimsical mood.

When Evel emerged from hospital, he decided to up the ante again. He announced his intention of jumping over the Grand Canyon. He kept his hand in, meanwhile, by breaking his right leg and foot in May (five months after the Caesar's Palace spectacular) and his hip in October.

It became clear that nobody was going to let this lunatic jump the Grand Canyon, so he announced that, in September 1972, he'd be jumping the Snake River Canyon.

In May 1971 he jumped over thirteen Pepsi trucks, scoring a crowd-pleasing compound fracture to the right arm, and breaking both legs and his collarbone. The following March, he managed to fall off and be run over by his own motorbike, suffering a broken back and concussion.

That put the schedule for the Snake River jump back a bit, but when Evel finally stayed out of hospital for long enough, a date – September 1974 – was set. Evel would not be using a normal motorcycle. No. For this jump, he'd be strapped into a special 'Skycycle' with a booster rocket powered by superheated steam. The State of Idaho officially classified it as an aeroplane.

That may be why – despite the jump being the predictable cock-up (his parachute deployed as he left the take-off ramp, and the wind blew him back into the canyon; he landed at the bottom) – Evel, on this occasion, sustained only minor injuries.

In 1975, he announced his retirement – walking out of Wembley Stadium with a broken pelvis after another landing proved a partial success. 'I walked in,' he said. 'I want to walk out.'

* * *

Erratum slip from the US edition of the book *Easy Sky Diving*: 'Please make the following correction: On page 8 line 7 "State zip code" should read "Pull rip cord".'

* * *

In Autumn 2007, eighty-five volunteers from twelve countries across Europe gathered in Holland for an attempt on the world record for the greatest number of dominoes toppled with a single push.

It took them eight weeks of full-time work to stand 4.5 million dominoes on their ends. A huge clock counted down, and with a roar of approval, the British singer Katie Melua tipped over the first domino. 3,671,465 of the dominoes fell – and then the chain broke in a fiddly section going over a bridge. They were about 300,000 dominoes short of the record. 'When you work eight weeks,' said their organizer, 'eight hours a day, five days a week... and your result is a loss, it's hard.'

Katie Melua, who had not been standing dominoes, was more upbeat: 'Just the experience of it was incredible.'

The laureate of domino disappointment, though, is Bob Specas. In June 1978 at the Manhattan Center in New York he was within an ace of breaking the domino-toppling world record – having posed 97,499 of the 100,000 dominoes he intended to topple. A TV cameraman on hand to record the historic event dropped his press badge and set the whole lot off prematurely.

* * *

In 1999, a Thai man who fancied himself as a snake-charmer was summoned to a neighbour's house in the southern province of Uttradit to help them dispose of a python that had found its way indoors. He emerged from the house with a big grin and a burlap sack containing the five-foot snake.

Encouraged by the admiring villagers to show them his quarry, he pulled the snake out and put it round his neck. It strangled him to death on the spot.

* * *

An academic paper entitled 'A Case of Fatal Suffocation During an Attempt to Swallow a Pool Ball' tells the story of a 23-year-old Edinburgh man whose party trick in the pub was to appear to swallow balls from the pool table to impress his mates.

The trick to this is to hold the pool ball in the back of your throat, nestled neatly against your pharynx. A standard pool ball – 50.3 mm in diameter – was just the right size for our man to do that.

On this particular night, his hand alighted on the cue-ball

– which being slightly smaller at 47.5 mm across was just the right size to slot neatly into the back of his throat and lodge there snugly, cutting off his air supply.

He turned blue, collapsed and died outside the pub. The man was described by police as 'of low intelligence'.

SOD AND GOD

The Rev. Philip Randall, a vicar and amateur antiquarian, spent eight years combing parish records to track down the identity of the person with the initials 'H. W. P.' who lay buried in his Peterborough churchyard. He eventually established that the initials stood for 'Hot Water Pipe'.

* * *

'Prepare for rebirth, ye faithful, and follow me,' were the last words of Pastor Michael Davis of the Larose Christian Fellowship Church, as he stripped to his swimming trunks and stepped into the municipal pool where he was preparing to baptise twelve members of his flock.

There was a loud bang, and Pastor Davis floated, stone dead, to the surface of the pool. The microphone he carried into the water was not properly earthed.

'It's just as well no one did follow him,' was the judgement of one onlooker.

* * *

Elizabeth Grumpin was trapped for five hours underneath a gravestone that toppled over while she was paying her respects to her two deceased sisters. Her husband explained that the incident had been particularly upsetting because 'my wife's nephew was crushed to death by a similar grave-stone two years ago'.

* * *

'It is true that Arthur Mage was a homeless alcoholic who made well over a hundred appearances before the bench. However, he once gave me the most perfect definition of Christian life,' said Dr Michael Avon at Mage's Cambridge memorial service in 1978. 'Unfortunately it was some years ago and I have lost the piece of paper on which I jotted it down.'

* * *

The Bible being one of the few books in which a printing error can imperil the immortal souls of millions of people, Sod's Law has paid its compositors particular attention over the years.

'I knew the tyme when great care was had about printing,' grumbled a seventeenth-century Archbishop of Canterbury, 'the Bibles especially, good compositors and the best correctors were gotten being grave and learned men, the paper and the letter rare, and faire every way of the beste, but now the paper is nought, the composers boyes, and the correctors unlearned.'

Most 'unlearned' of all were undoubtedly the correctors on the so-called 'Wicked Bible' of 1631, published by the royal printers Robert Barker and Martin Lucas. What was intended to be a straightforward reprint of the King James version went critically wrong with the accidental omission of an important 'not'. Exodus 20:14, therefore, told the faithful: 'Thou shalt commit adultery.'

Missing out a word is one thing. But how the printers came to misspell the word 'greatness' quite so badly in Deuteronomy 5:24 continues to beggar the imagination. 'The Lord,' it announced, 'hath shewed us his glory and his great arse.'

A furious Charles I ordered all copies recalled and burned (only eleven survive today), and the printers hauled before the Star Chamber. They were discouraged from continuing their publishing career.

A quarter-century later, another missing 'not' gave encouragement to sinners, when a 1653 edition asked: 'Know ye not that the unrighteous shall inherit the Kingdom of God?' An edition in 1716 had Christ inviting his flock to 'Go and sin on more.' A 1763 Bible told readers – another of those pesky missing negatives – 'the fool hath said in his heart there is a God'.

Other editions have introduced a 'Parable of the Vinegar' where the devout were expecting a vineyard, an additional miracle ('thy son that shall come forth out of thy lions'), an underwhelming Creation ('the first heaven and the first earth were passed away and there was more sea') and have wondered whether Gilead contains treacle.

Some mistakes are deliberate, however. Surely the misprint for 'princes' in a pre-1700 edition of the Bible was the work of a disgruntled typesetter – Psalms 119:161: 'Printers have persecuted me without cause.'

* * *

In 1625, after ninety years of labour by the most skilled and devout workmen the area could muster, the Church of Corcuetos in Navarette, Spain was completed. It fell down the following day.

* * *

The Hindu god Ganesha is one of a relatively small number of divine instances of Sod's Law in action. Not long after his birth, so some versions of the legend have it, he was snuggled up in bed with his mother Parvati when his father Shiva arrived home from a journey.

Confronted by the spectacle of a strange young man in his wife's bed (Ganesha, being divine, was born adolescent), Shiva whipped out his trident and smartly decapitated the interloper.

'Now look what you've done!' said Parvati, or words to that effect. Thinking fast – but not, Ganesha might have reflected later, fast enough – Shiva performed some emergency surgery, gluing the head of a passing elephant onto his son's body. Ganesha has had an elephant bonce ever since.

* * *

In May 1975, 125,000 people gathered in the centre of Washington DC to celebrate 'Human Kindness Day'. The highlight of the day was a concert at the Washington Monument with Stevie Wonder at the top of the bill, and the organizers – a charity called Compared To What – anticipated a city-wide diffusion of good vibes, small acts of charity, and neighbourliness.

It did not work out precisely that way. A 22-year-old Austrian tourist standing near the base of the monument had his wallet stolen and was hit in the mouth with a club. An 18-year-old out-of-towner was set upon by twenty youths who beat and bottled him until he escaped to an ambulance, and a third man was stabbed in the eye while passing through the festival of goodwill on his way home from work.

'I said "Help me!",' he told the *Washington Post* afterwards, 'and there was no response.'

Violent gangs of kindness enthusiasts surged through the crowd, terrorizing spectators, committing acts of racist violence, and 'often stampeding the crowd before them like tightly packed sheep'. It turned into a fully fledged riot, with the 262 unarmed volunteer marshals who were in charge of security struggling to control the 124,738 high-spirited altruists.

'People were blindly grabbing handbags,' Officer Kenneth Donovan of Washington's Parks Police reported. 'It got to be a thing to grab open a woman's blouse and rip it and run.' The police only refrained from using tear gas because they feared it would cause the violence to spread downtown.

At a press conference after the event, the police announced that Human Kindness Day had seen 600 arrests, 500 robberies, 150 smashed windows, 120 occurrences of public brawling, 42 concession stands looted, 33 acts of arson, 17 attacks on police officers, and 14 cars completely destroyed.

A spokeswoman for the organizers said that 'although sporadic rock-throwing, public mayhem and purse-snatchings had been a sadness, a lot of beautiful things were going on out there.'

* * *

In September 1999, three terrorists were killed when – at precisely 5.30 p.m. Israel Standard Time – the car-bombs they were driving en route to their targets exploded prematurely while they were still inside.

The terrorists had failed to account for the fact that, three days previously, Israel had put the clocks back an hour to

Israel Standard Time. Refusing to live on 'Zionist time', the Palestinian territories were still on Daylight Savings.

The bomb-makers had armed the bombs to go off at half past five, their time. The drivers, with their targets in mind, had already adjusted their watches to the Israeli time zone.

Nobody else was hurt in the explosions.

* * *

A handsome lad – half human and half water-nymph on his mother's side – Tithonus seemed to have everything going for him, a lyre in his hand, the run of ancient Troy, and not a care in the world.

Then, like a humble heart surgeon copping off with the late Diana, Princess of Wales, Tithonus caught the fancy of Eos, the Goddess of the Dawn and the original rosy-fingered lovely. That being the way of god/mortal courtship in those days, she kidnapped him and took his brother Ganymede along for good measure.

Just as we are warned to beware Greeks bearing gifts, it pays to be very cautious indeed around Greek gods wanting to do you a favour. They invariably cock it up. So it was with Eos, who, contemplating their mortality mismatch, lobbied Zeus to grant her boyfriend eternal life.

Zeus, taking a fancy to the brother, did a swap. Eos handed over Ganymede in exchange for one wish. She wished for eternal life for Tithonus, and it was granted. Being a ditz, though, she forgot to include eternal youth in the package.

At first, according to the *Homeric Hymn to Aphrodite*, all was fine. He hung onto his adolescence and was to be found living at the ends of the earth and 'enjoying Eos, the one with the golden embroidery'.

But soon after the first grey hair appeared, Eos dumped

him. She kept him around to start with, for old time's sake. But when this wrinkly and strengthless old geezer became really unsightly, she bundled him into a back room and closed the shining doors of the dawn on him for good.

And there he's been ever since, vainly pleading to be allowed for God's sake to die. As Tennyson reminds us in his first-rate poem about Tithonus, though: 'The Gods themselves cannot recall their gifts.'

One version of the story has Tithonus shrivelling away until he becomes a cricket. Which is why if you listen carefully to a cicada, you can hear it saying 'Bugger it! Bugger it! Bugger it!'

* * *

'I have sad news for you,' a certain gentlewoman announced, on being received into the Irish novelist George Moore's study. 'I regret to inform you that your friend Martin Ross is dead.' Moore fell immediately into an appropriate gloom.

'How sad,' he rumbled. 'How very sad.' He walked back and forth. 'How sad. Here I am in the midst of this, alive...' he gestured at the books and fine furnishings around him, 'and my friend, my dear friend Edmund Gosse, dead.'

'I beg your pardon, Mr Moore. It is Martin Ross, not Edmund Gosse.'

Moore, peevish: 'My dear woman. Surely you don't expect me to go through all that again?'

SOD AND PLOD

In November 1975, seventy-five convicts from Saltillo Prison in northern Mexico spent six months digging an escape tunnel that would pass right under the prison walls and – they quite reasonably imagined – bring them to freedom. In April of the following year, they broke through to the surface – and found themselves in the very courtroom in which many of them had received their initial sentences. The judge sent them promptly back to jail.

* * *

In 1978, a newsagent in Barking, Essex, determined to catch a thief who had persistently sneaked £10 from the till between late night and early morning. When he closed the shop for the night, he concealed himself in a large cardboard box, where he remained vigilant for fourteen hours without incident. He got up for a pee as dawn broke. When he returned to his box, he discovered that the thief had been and gone.

* * *

In the wee small hours of the morning, four men were spotted by a police patrol breaking into a Ford Capri. (This story, in the form it reaches me, must now be a few years old.

Who now sees a Ford Capri? And who on earth would steal one?) The patrolmen gave chase and a *Dukes of Hazzard*-style festival of burnt rubber ensued.

The Capri streaked off in the wrong direction down an isolated dual carriageway, veering from side to side and briefly mounting the footpath before returning to the road. With several units now in pursuit, the driver executed a handbrake turn and started back along the carriageway, scattering his pursuers. Shortly afterwards, though, tested beyond endurance, one of the car's front wheels came flying off and in a shower of sparks the car ploughed to a halt.

The coppers duly nicked the four thieves. It was only as they were doing so that they became aware of a suspicious figure, a hundred yards away or so up the road, emerging from the dark shadows of a hedge. He was limping, bruised and wearing a once-smart suit now covered in mud.

The patrolmen asked him what he was up to. He had been gambling in a casino in Southend with his girlfriend, he said, and lost his whole stack. A drunkenly enthusiastic attempt to reason with the casino management had resulted in his being thrown out, at which point he and his girlfriend had started having a row.

The final word in this row had been hers. She had driven off in his car and left him stranded without money or credit cards. He had been in the process of walking home along the side of the dual carriageway when a Ford Capri had come careering out of nowhere onto the footpath and within an ace of killing him. He had jumped into the hedge and stayed there until it had seemed safe to come out.

Just as he was continuing on his way, he had been stricken by the sight of the same car coming at him again from the opposite direction. It had whooshed past noisily, to his great relief, 'and then I saw this tyre coming at me...'

* * *

In June 2007, the Irish police force finally caught up with Prawo Jazdy, a reckless driver who had racked up more than fifty motoring offences across the Republic. In each case, Mr Jazdy had given the arresting officers a false address and absconded without paying a fine.

'Prawo Jazdy is actually the Polish for "driving licence" and not the first and surname on the licence,' wrote the explanatory letter circulated by an officer working in the Garda's traffic division.

'Having noticed this, I decided to check and see how many times officers have made this mistake. It is quite embarrassing to see that the system has created Prawo Jazdy as a person with over fifty identities.'

* * *

The death of Thai gambler Dam Saeng Dung at a card game with friends came as a surprise to all concerned. Halfway through the game police burst into the deserted hut where they were sitting on the outskirts of Bangkok, and shot Mr Dung dead.

The police were there at Mr Dung's invitation. He wanted them to arrest his fellow card player Vichien Benjawan, whom he believed to have stolen his watch. A police spokesman said: 'We have apologized to Mr Dung's family. When Mr Dung informed us of his rendezvous with the notorious thief Benjawan, he unfortunately enclosed a photograph of himself rather than the criminal.'

* * *

In 1975, a light-fingered Yarmouth man stole a sheepskin jacket from the lobby of a hotel. The passing coach from which he subsequently thumbed a lift, he was dismayed to discover, was carrying forty Detective Chief Inspectors of Police on their way from a seminar. The thief had been in the coach for no longer than two minutes when one of the Detective Chief Inspectors recognized his sheepskin jacket.

'I realized that I had made a terrible mistake,' our man said afterwards.

* * *

A pair of North Walean lads were arrested at their homes in Anglesey, having been identified as the thugs who had pulled their car over on a country road and beaten up a couple of smartly dressed pedestrians at random.

They explained themselves quite cogently. They confirmed that they had been involved in the incident, but had acted in self-defence. They had been driving home quite complacently when the supposed victims had jumped out in front of them. Having swerved to avoid a collision, they stopped their car – only to be set upon by these drunken strangers. Using only enough violence to ensure their safe escape, they had set off again for home.

The constable interviewing them read from one of the victims' witness statements: 'As part of our training to enter the priesthood, it is necessary to visit local parishioners...'

* * *

Presiding in Bow Street Magistrates' Court, Sir James Ingham, the Chief Metropolitan Magistrate of London, was presented with two men in a state of extreme agitation. Both plaintiff and defendant had been travelling together in a closed railway carriage, and the plaintiff had nodded off. On waking, he noticed that his watch and chain were nowhere to be found.

Despite the defendant's protestations of innocence, the plaintiff had him arrested on arrival at Waterloo. The watch was not found on him, but Sir James – discovering that while at Waterloo another man had briefly become involved (he'd wanted to know what the matter was) – guessed that it had been passed to this confederate.

He remanded the defendant – yelping with indignation – into custody. The trial was scheduled for the following day. The plaintiff arrived in court crimson with shame. On arriving home, he'd discovered that he had left his watch on the bedside table and had never had it in the train in the first place. An innocent man had been locked up.

Sir James was full of worldly fellow-feeling, and made a point of telling the court what an easy mistake it was to make. 'Why, by an extraordinary coincidence, this very morning I made the same error myself. I dressed in a hurry and, after leaving my house in Kensington, discovered I'd left my watch at home.'

He duly discharged the poor defendant, amid much apologizing from the plaintiff, and got on with the day's business. That evening he returned home and was greeted by his daughter.

'Did you get your watch all right, Papa?'

'Actually, I left it at home this morning.'

'I know, Papa. I gave it to the man from Bow Street who called to pick it up.'

* * *

When in 1975 Indiana State's biggest prison, 'Whitehill', advertised for a senior medical adviser, their appointments board was overwhelmingly impressed by one applicant, 53-year-old Dr R. H. Hales. 'Dr Hales gave a brilliant interview,' the head of the board said. They unhesitatingly appointed him to the post at a salary of $35,000 per year.

He remained in post – discharging his duties, we must assume, satisfactorily – until his photograph appeared in the local newspaper. At that point he was returned to 'Byeways', Indiana State's biggest asylum, from which he had escaped two days before applying for his job.

* * *

In 2002, two enterprising pranksters spotted a Krispy Kreme doughnut truck idling in the parking lot of a Louisiana convenience store. While the driver was inside making his delivery, they hijacked the truck and roared off in the direction of the nearby town of Lacombe, rubbing their tummies like Yogi Bear in receipt of a pickernick basket.

They were disconcerted, said 31-year-old Rose Houk – who bashfully admitted that they'd been smoking crack 'for hours' before the incident – when the police caught up with them. They had not realized that the rear doors of the truck were open throughout their getaway, and they had left a 15-mile-long trail of doughnuts along the highway.

* * *

Contrary to Hollywood myth, Bonnie and Clyde's bank-robbing career was – in the words of their biographer Jeff Guinn – 'more a reign of error than a reign of terror'.

Early in Clyde Barrow's criminal career, for instance, he

and a couple of confederates broke into a railroad depot in southwest Ohio. Clyde's crude attempt to case the place – and the fact that the gang kept their stolen car parked outside all afternoon – meant that the ticket agent had already written the car's number plate down and handed it to police before they committed a crime.

When darkness fell, Clyde and his pals broke in, grabbed $60, and hauled off on an unpaved country road, anxious to get out of town and lie low. They almost immediately got lost, and were forced to spend the night in the car.

The next morning found two officers of the Middletown police force at the railroad depot, taking down the details of the crime, and writing the number of the suspicious car in their pads. One of them looked up to see a car bearing that very number plate chugging past the depot with three puzzled-looking men squinting out of the window.

Still completely lost, Clyde and his confederates had blundered back to the scene of the crime. They were promptly arrested.

This sort of automative misfortune was to bedevil Clyde's career. He and his cigar-chomping moll were perpetually running out of petrol, suffering a flat battery, or sinking up to their axles in mud and having to flee on foot.

That wasn't so easy for them either. While in custody, Clyde chopped off two of his own toes with an axe in the hopes of being invalided out of the punishing labour regime of Eastham Farm penitentiary. He needn't have bothered. Five days after the amputation, the news came through that he had been paroled.

Bonnie, by the end, could travel on foot only by hopping: Clyde – barrelling as ever through the night in a stolen car – had driven them directly into a riverbed at top speed, having not noticed the 'Detour' sign where a bridge was being built.

Acid from the car battery had burned one of Bonnie's legs down to the bone.

They stole, as often as not, cash registers with barely a dollar in them, and had a particular knack for knocking off banks where the safes were empty, the bank tellers heavily armed, or the police nearby.

The nadir of Clyde's criminal career came when one of his gang got beaten up by grannies.

Clyde and two other members of the gang (Bonnie was not on hand to witness this humiliating incident) were being chased all over Oklahoma by the police, and Clyde stole four different cars in a single day in the hopes of losing them.

In the countryside of northern Oklahoma, the fourth car got – as they always seemed to – irretrievably bogged down in mud. Clyde and his felonious pals – Henry Massingale and Dock Potter – had to hike into the nearest town.

'At one house they saw some elderly women playing croquet in the front yard,' writes Guinn. 'Massingale ran up to them, waved a .45, and demanded the keys to one of the cars parked along the kerb. Instead of giving him the keys, two of the ladies began whacking Massingale with their croquet mallets. Someone called the town police, and the battered crook was arrested.'

* * *

In 1978, a Philadelphia car alarm salesman by the name of Ray Wright had the idea of promoting his business by leaving fliers underneath the windscreen wipers of parked cars. 'If you didn't see me put this on your windshield,' they read, 'I could just as easily have stolen your car.' While he was leafleting cars, his truck was stolen.

* * *

In 1977, Clive Bunyan leaped off his motorbike and stormed into a North Yorkshire village shop armed with a toy pistol and wearing a full-face crash helmet as a disguise. He persuaded the 15-year-old shop assistant to hand over the contents of the till, before roaring off on his motorbike with £157 in cash. His motorbike helmet, as the police were pleased to discover, had the words 'Clive Bunyan: Driver' in inch-high letters across the front.

* * *

At around teatime on 3 February 1990, David Zaback strolled into a crowded shop in Washington State in the north-west of the United States. He pulled out a .38-calibre semi-automatic pistol and announced that this was a robbery and he'd shoot dead anybody who didn't put their hands on the counter and keep them there.

His instructions were disregarded. Several of the customers, a shop assistant and a policeman immediately drew guns and invited him to make their day – which he promptly did,

The mistake he made, as he would have had cause to reflect afterwards had he not been lying dead with three bullets in the chest and one in his arm, was that the shop he chose to try and rob was called 'H. & J. Leather and Firearms Limited'. The clue was in the name.

Actually, that wasn't his only mistake. His other mistake was deciding to rob the shop while Timothy Lally, a policeman with eighteen years experience on the force, was leaning up against the counter having a coffee and shooting the breeze with the owner of the gun shop.

Mr Lally was in uniform at the time.

'The surprising thing,' Police Captain Don Persson told reporters afterwards, 'is that the man had to walk right past a marked police car to get in the front door.'

* * *

In summer 1999, a pickpocket working Seville Airport picked out a likely mark in the form of a lanky looking lad on the fringes of a group of young men. He dipped the fellow's bag and legged it.

The victim, unfortunately for our hero, was Larry Wade, a champion US hurdler – and his team-mate Maurice Green spotted the theft. Two months previously, Mr Green had broken the world record for the 100-metre dash – 9.79 seconds.

Collared faster than he knew what was happening, the thief protested his innocence... until it became clear that the whole series of events had been captured by the film crew who were interviewing Mr Green at the time.

* * *

Twenty-two-year-old Myner Santiago Martinez of Anaheim, California, broke into the Los Angeles home of Luis Gasca at 3 a.m. on a Sunday morning, armed with a knife. How was he to know that Mr Gasca was a serving officer with the LAPD? And that he kept his gun with him in bed?

When the first shot rang out, Martinez took to his toes. Those toes carried him out of the window and face down into Mr Gasca's prized bed of cactuses. Bristling with agonizing cactus spines, he got to his feet and attempted to hurdle the ornate wrought-iron fence – which speared him viciously in the private parts.

He was arrested later when he presented himself at the hospital seeking treatment for 'cuts, abrasions, and a groin injury that he couldn't explain'.

* * *

A man bailed on suspicion of assault turned up at a Devon police station in order to take part in an identification parade. This man knew that the case against him was thin, had a good solicitor at his side, and every confidence of acquittal.

At the line-up, he took care to stand between the two other people who looked most like him. The witness, an elderly woman, entered the room. She paused, fished her glasses out of her handbag, and perched them on her nose.

'She wasn't wearing those the other day!' the man exclaimed.

On the advice of his solicitor, he later changed his plea.

* * *

During the miners' strike in eighties' Britain, there were frequent and bitter clashes between the lines of police, brought in from all over the country, and lines of striking miners, in many cases likewise on an away-day. Flying pickets versus flying pigs, you might think of it.

High tempers, and flying half-bricks, can affect the self-control of even the most disciplined coppers. It became clear at one point that a particular police division, from Walsall in the West Midlands, was making charges into the crowd on its own initiative rather than the orders of its commanding officer.

Turning to face his men and reassert control, the officer struggled to make himself heard. 'If any of you breaks ranks again without my direct order,' he shouted, 'I will put you on a charge!'

'CHARGE!' repeated the conveniently hard-of-hearing PCs, rushing forward as one and flattening him.

* * *

Police arriving at the scene of a burglary – there had been reports of a knife-wielding intruder at the premises – caught sight of a frenzied male figure running out of the door. They gunned the car and ran him over, breaking his leg.

As he lay howling in agony, they nicked him. 'Call me an ambulance,' he begged. 'You're an ambulance,' sneered one of the officers.

It presently became apparent that the man on the ground was not the burglar, but the owner of the house.

* * *

It was just gone closing time when traffic police, staking out the car park of a busy pub on a Friday night, saw a likely suspect emerge. The man, so drunk he could barely stand up, tumbled out of the door into the car park.

He spent a good five minutes trying to find his car, another five fishing his keys out of his pocket, and another five trying to fit them into the door lock. Eventually, with a great cough, the car started up, roared, hopped forward and stalled. It coughed into life again, made wobbly progress towards the entrance of the car park and out onto the main road, where it crawled along in the dark for thirty seconds before the driver even remembered to turn the lights on.

The cops set the blue lights and sirens going, pulled the car over and breathalysed the driver. The reading showed completely clear. They asked the driver to accompany them to the station for a urine test, on the grounds that the breathalyser was obviously broken.

'I'm not sure it is, officer,' the driver said grinning broadly. 'I'm tonight's designated decoy.'

* * *

A silky defence barrister with a client convicted for fraud made a plea ahead of sentencing. The defendant accepted that his actions had been wrong, had shown due contrition, and could in no way be regarded as a threat to society. 'If – and I stress "if" – Your Honour is considering a custodial sentence, I beg to suggest it be numbered in months, rather than years.'

'I hear what you say, and am happy to accept your suggestion,' the judge said in due course. 'I sentence your client to seventy-two months' imprisonment.'

THE ART OF LOSING

In an effort to recreate the televisual magic of Groucho Marx's *You Bet Your Life*, the American network CBS screened the premiere of an exciting new game show in January 1961.

You're in the Picture was hosted by the bumptious comedian Jackie Gleason. The rules were simple. Celebrity guests would stick their heads through life-sized panels of famous scenes, and try to guess what the picture was of by asking Gleason questions.

The show, unfortunately, was an epic flop – such a disaster that some conspiracy theorists believed it had been done deliberately. Nobody had the first idea what picture they were in, and neither host, panellist or audience seemed to care.

The second show was markedly different in format. Gleason – by pointing out that the show had had sponsors – disabused viewers of the hope it had been done deliberately. It really had been as bad as they thought, and it really had been an accident.

'Ladies and gentlemen,' he said, 'I think you'll notice that there is no panel tonight.' Instead, the whole thirty-minute show was giving over to Gleason, sitting on a bare stage, swigging from a mug that, he assured viewers, was 'chock full o' booze' and musing on the 'intangibles of show business' that had led him to this sorry pass.

The programme, he said, had had nearly three hundred

years of showbiz experience behind it – and yet had 'laid the biggest bomb in history... this would make the H-bomb look like a two-inch salute... you don't have to be Alexander Graham Bell to pick up a phone and know it's dead.'

His apology was so successful that the show was renamed *The Jackie Gleason Show*. It ran on and off for eighteen years.

* * *

'ABSOLUTELY FIREPROOF' was what it said in capital letters at the top of the playbills for the matinee performance of *Mr Bluebeard*, the first play ever to be performed at Chicago's new Iroquois Theatre. You can guess what happened next, can't you?

It was 1903, and the new theatre was the pride of the Windy City – intended to rival New York for glamour and sophistication. It was opened in something of a rush, though, and 'Absolutely Fireproof' might have better read 'Theatre-Sized Tinderbox: Take Your Chances'.

The interior was almost entirely made of wood, the fire escapes had not been finished, there was no fire alarm, and the total fire-fighting equipment – no doubt on the grounds that it would never be needed – consisted of just six canisters of a powder extinguisher called Kilfyre. There were no exit signs, the theatre's architect later explained, because he 'thought they would spoil the look'.

The theatre's capacity was 1,602. On 30 December, 1,840 people showed up for the matinee, and were admitted. The doors, which opened inwards, were locked and bolted.

During the big musical number in Act II, a light above the stage shorted and set fire to the drapery. The cast stayed in character. The stagehand who was usually in charge of the fire curtain was, unluckily, off sick and his replacement didn't know how to operate it. When they finally managed to lower it, it got stuck.

The lead actor, Eddie Foy, advised the audience: 'Don't be frightened, go slow, walk out calmly, take your time.'

The cast left character and fled through the scenery doors at the back of the building. Opening these doors had the effect of causing an enormous backdraught that instantly incinerated those who had taken Mr Foy's advice.

The sensible stampeders who had managed to find an unlocked door found themselves on a platform high above the alley behind the building. Had the fire escape been completed, the platform would have been connected to the ground by a ladder. It was not.

A ladder was produced from the building opposite and extended to bridge the gap. The first man who stepped on it slipped and tumbled to the cobblestones below, taking the ladder with him. The fire brigade showed up and encouraged the remaining people to jump down into the nets they were holding. Thanks to the thick smoke, this tactic had distinctly mixed results. The following day, 125 bodies were recovered from the alleyway.

It was the worst single-building disaster in US fire-fighting history. Six hundred people were killed. 'THE IROQUOIS FIRE HORROR' was what it said in capital letters at the top of the *Chicago Daily News*.

* * *

'We poets in our youth begin in gladness,' wrote Wordsworth, 'but thereof comes in the end despondency and madness.' This is understandable. Writing poetry is a lonely and difficult task, selling it is next to impossible, and reading from it in public can be exactly as lonely as writing it.

The poet Simon Armitage describes fleeing the scene of a typically dispiriting reading – somnolent audience members, a compère who doesn't know who he is, a night listening to amateur poetry in a pube-ridden bedsit – and passing time in the precinct of the railway station while waiting for a train home.

In a second-hand bookshop he notices a first edition of one of his own books. It is marked 'Signed' and costs 10p. He opens it. Underneath the signature, in his own handwriting, are the words: 'To Mum and Dad'.

George Bernard Shaw, incidentally, offers an example of how to deal with this sort of indignity. He came across a copy of one of his books in a bookshop, inscribed in his own hand: 'To X with esteem, George Bernard Shaw'. He bought it and gave it back to X, amending the inscription to read: 'To X with renewed esteem, George Bernard Shaw'.

Wordsworth, on the other hand, became Poet Laureate, giving him high public status and ample financial security. He lived to a ripe old age.

* * *

Algernon Swinburne, though a decent enough poet, was a rotter as a houseguest. When staying as a guest of the Master of Balliol College, Oxford – an eminent classicist by the name of Jowett – he cast an eye over his host's translation of Plato and immediately suggested a correction.

The Master, on the back foot: 'Of course that is the meaning. You would be a good scholar if you were to study.' Jowett received another guest, and Swinburne drifted into the next room, nose still in the Plato.

An occasional stagy yelp of laughter could be heard through the door. 'Another howler, Master!' Swinburne called merrily.

'Thank you, dear Algernon,' Jowett replied, pushing the door firmly to.

* * *

The great actor Sir Donald Wolfit was noted for his somewhat high-handed treatment of more junior members of the company.

He had cast one ambitious younger actor, for season after season and obdurately ignoring pleas for bigger parts, as the spear-carrier Seyton in *Macbeth* – a character who has fewer than fifty words to speak in the whole play.

Six of those words are quite important, though. When Wolfit's Macbeth exclaims 'Wherefore was that cry?', Seyton reports: 'The queen, my lord, is dead.'

At this point, Macbeth launches into an impassioned and grief-stricken soliloquy about the meaninglessness of life: 'Tomorrow, and tomorrow, and tomorrow/ Creeps in this petty pace…'

On the final night of the run, Wolfit delivered his line. Seyton appeared on stage and with a broad grin announced: 'The queen, my lord, is much, *much* better!' He walked offstage, out of the theatre's back door, and was never heard from again.

* * *

In early 1993, the novelist Rupert Thomson was wintering in a farmhouse in Siena with his partner Kate. Every ten years, the literary magazine *Granta* announces its Best of Young British Novelists, a list of twenty writers under forty it tips for future superstardom. It was due to announce its 1993 list that spring, and Thomson was eligible.

While tearing up newspapers to light a fire, Kate chanced on a small black-and-white photograph of Thomson accompanying an article about the announcement. She ran upstairs waving the paper and told him he'd made the list.

Thomson, feverish with excitement, scanned the article for his name. It did not appear. His partner had mistaken his face for Jeanette Winterson's.

* * *

The American novelist Rick Moody was once described by a critic as 'the worst writer of his generation'. 'I apologize for the abruptness of this declaration, its lack of nuance, of any meaning besides the intuitive,' wrote the critic in question, Dale Peck, 'but as I made my way through Moody's oeuvre during the past few months I was unable to come up with any other starting point for a consideration of his accomplishment.'

Mr Moody arranged to settle his differences with Mr Peck by throwing a custard pie into his face.

Mr Peck's view is not shared by everyone. Mr Moody reports that his own mother used to review his work online: 'She once reviewed a book by me on Amazon.com and gave me three out of five stars.'

He added: 'Then she told me it was a *positive* review.'

* * *

The actor who muffs his lines is a perennial joy in the theatre. Few muff them so inventively as the legendary thespian who was required to exclaim: 'Hark! I hear a pistol shot!'

Onstage, he declared: 'Hark! I hear a shostel pit! A shistel pot! A postel shit! Oh shit, I'm shot! Oh fuck, I'm fired.'

* * *

In April 2009, the punk-rock pioneer Iggy Pop (James Osterberg, Jr to his mother) had what observers would identify as his least punk-rock moment ever. In a career that saw him being arrested for drug possession and indecent exposure, surfing into crowds with his chest bleeding from self-inflicted lacerations, and displaying his generously pro-portioned private parts to complete strangers at the slightest provocation, he was... given a mild ticking off by the Advertising Standards Authority.

Mr Pop – having made the inevitable journey from Stooge to stooge – had appeared in an advertisement for a car insurance company called Swiftcover, in which he had announced to an apathetic nation: 'I'm Swiftcovered! I've got insurance on my insurance!'

This, presumably, was intended to convey that even if you have the sort of drug-addled, wild and crazy rock lifestyle of an Iggy Pop, you can still get insured up to the hilt with Swiftcover. Unfortunately, as the ASA was swift to point out, Iggy didn't have insurance on his insurance. He didn't even have insurance, because Swiftcover's policy terms specifically bar them from taking on anyone who works in the entertainment industry, let alone mentally questionable pharmacological disaster areas like Mr Pop.

The company afterwards said that the advert had been 'a great success'.

* * *

In 1996, the beer company Molson staged a series of rock concerts in order to raise the profile of its brand. The results were mixed. Chris Cornell of Soundgarden announced to the

crowd: 'We're here because of some beer company...
LABATT'S!'

Courtney Love got the name of the beer right. 'God bless
Molson,' she said. 'I douche with it every day.'

* * *

After the 1922 premiere of Igor Stravinsky's one-act chamber
opera *Renard*, Marcel Proust approached the composer to
offer his congratulations. It was the opportunity for a
meeting of minds between two of the most innovative artists
of the twentieth century.

The conversation went like this.

> Proust: 'Do you like Beethoven?'
> Stravinsky: 'I detest him.'
> Proust: 'But the late quartets?'
> Stravinsky: 'Worst thing he ever wrote.'
> Proust: '...'

Stravinsky later explained that, actually, he did like
Beethoven well enough but 'it was a commonplace among
intellectuals of that time' to praise him, and he didn't want
to do the predictable thing.

* * *

The great American novelist William Faulkner had a robust
attitude to paid employment. He was relieved of his position
at the University of Mississippi post office after complaining
that his recreational reading was being interrupted by 'any
son-of-a-bitch who has two cents to buy a stamp'.

* * *

In December 1932, W. B. Yeats was a guest at a dinner in Wellesley College in Massachusetts. As the evening wound on, Yeats fell into an involving conversation about poetry with his next-door neighbour. It was late in the meal before he realized he'd addressed not a word to the fellow on his other side.

'My friend here and I,' he said jovially, 'have been discussing the defects of T. S. Eliot's poetry. What do you think of the poetry?'

The man pursed his lips slightly, and wordlessly held his place card up for Yeats to read. It said: 'T. S. Eliot'.

* * *

'Who will, may hear Sordello's story told'.

With this line, Robert Browning opened the long poem that he was convinced would at last make him famous. The public had not responded to *Paracelsus* with the rapture he had hoped, so he had deliberately written something he reckoned would have more popular appeal.

He was sadly wrong. *Sordello* – six thousand lines of densely allegorical poetry about the nature of poetry, expressed through a complex analogy involving the thirteenth-century war in northern Italy between the Guelphs and the Ghibbelines (Who they? Well you might ask.) and with no punctuation used to indicate direct speech – is routinely described as the least comprehensible poem in the English language.

The present author can attest to that. I've actually read the bastard. I still have no idea what it's all about. Thomas Carlyle's wife Jane – by reputation at least the equal of her husband in literary matters – read it through and declared that she'd been unable to discover whether Sordello was a man, a city or a book.

The playwright Douglas Jerrold tried to read *Sordello* while recovering from a serious illness, and found it so bewildering he became convinced that he'd become insane. The actor William Charles Macready recorded in his diary for 17 June 1840: 'After dinner tried – another attempt – utterly desperate – on *Sordello*: it is not readable.'

Alfred Tennyson declared that the only bits he'd been able to understand were the first line – announcing that Sordello's story was about to be told – and the last one, announcing that it had been. He judged both of them to have been lies.

'When I wrote that, God and I alone knew what it meant,' Browning said, years later when asked to explain a particular passage. He squinted at it. 'Now God alone knows.'

* * *

The Italian composer Pietro Mascagni was irritated beyond endurance one day, when he heard an organ-grinder outside the house where he was staying playing selections from his opera *Cavalleria Rusticana*.

Flattered though he was by the organ-grinder's choice of music, he was enraged by the sluggish tempo at which it was being played. Unable to bear it any longer, Mascagni rushed into the street, elbowed the organ-grinder aside, and, grabbing the handle of the organ, cranked it frantically until the music picked up a bit of speed.

The next week the organ-grinder was back on his rounds. There was a sign affixed to the organ saying: 'Pupil of Pietro Mascagni'.

* * *

For a 1949 production of *Don Giovanni* in Edinburgh, the conductor Rafael Kubelik came up with a novel means of balancing the acoustics. In order to give an appropriately otherworldly sound to the Commendatore's admonitions from beyond the grave (in Act II there's a talking statue in a graveyard; this sort of thing is commonplace in opera) he discovered that the perfect place to position the bass who was singing it, David Franklin, was in the gentlemen's lavatories between the green room and the stage.

There, along with three trombones, Mr Franklin was stationed, his ghostly tones echoing into the auditorium as if from the other side. On the first night of the performance, he was just intoning his ominous opening words 'Di rider finirai pria dell'aurora' ('This night shall see the end of all your laughter') when, as Hugh Vickers puts it in his *Great Operatic Disasters*, 'a mechanical system in the King's Theatre actually carried out its allotted task. The long-defunct automatic flush system suddenly came torrentially to life.'

The performance, as Sod of course had ensured, was being broadcast live on the BBC's Third Programme. A nation of opera-lovers listened to the ghostly voice of the Commendatore accompanied not by a trio of trombones, but by a heroically gushing five-urinal salute.

* * *

Probably the greatest literary hard-luck story of all time is that of the writing of *Kubla Khan*, Samuel Taylor Coleridge's epically trippy but altogether-shorter-than-he'd-intended piece of oriental mysticism.

The poem came to him whole in a dream, he claimed, after he'd fallen asleep over *Purchas, His Pilgrimage...* – an early seventeenth-century travel book compiled by an English clergyman named Samuel Purchas.

It was the summer of 1797, and Coleridge was then 'in ill health', as he put it. He had retired to a lonely farm-house on Exmoor to recover. We must read between the lines of his explanation, written in the third person, that, on this particular day, 'in consequence of a slight indisposition, an anodyne had been prescribed, from the effects of which he fell asleep in his chair'. Coleridge seldom had at his fingertips expressions like 'raving opium fiend', or 'on the nod'.

The sentence he was reading when his happy eyes rolled back in their sockets was: 'Here the Khan Kubla commanded a palace to be built, and a stately garden thereunto. And thus ten miles of fertile ground were inclosed with a wall.'

In his opium dream, it inspired the lines which were to go on to inspire artists as diverse as Olivia Newton-John and Frankie Goes to Hollywood: 'In Xanadu did Kubla Khan a stately pleasure dome decree...'

Coleridge claimed in the note he prefixed to the 1816 edition that in this dream he effortlessly composed not less than two- to three hundred lines of the poem – 'if that indeed can be called composition in which all the images rose up before him as *things*, with a parallel production of the correspondent expressions, without any sensation or consciousness of effort. On awaking he appeared to himself to have a distinct recollection of the whole, and taking his pen, ink and paper instantly and eagerly wrote down the lines that are here preserved.'

This is the sort of thing any poet dreams of: your best work, composed automatically and with no effort, while having a snooze. This was the point at which, of course, he was 'unfortunately called out by a person on business from Porlock'. By the time he had seen off his unwanted visitor, the major part of his best poem had vanished from his memory: 'though he still retained some vague and dim recollection of the general purport of the vision, yet, with the exception of some eight or ten scattered lines and images, all the rest had passed away like the images on the surface of a stream into which a stone has been cast, but, alas! without the restoration of the latter!'

Some questions have arisen, over the years, as to the identity of this Person from Porlock. Was this person male or female? Who on earth would plausibly have had 'business' with the whacked out hippie in the isolated farmhouse? Is it possible that the Porlockian visitor was also part of Coleridge's hallucination – a meta-hallucination, if you like? Or is it possible, as some have speculated, that the Person either never existed or was simply a convenient excuse for Coleridge having got stuck?

The eccentric poet Stevie Smith, writing much later, addressed just these questions in her excellent 'Thoughts About the Person from Porlock'. 'Why did he hurry to let him in?' she wondered. 'He could have just hid in the house.'

She concluded 'the truth is I think he was already stuck/ With Kubla Khan/ He was weeping and wailing: I am finished, finished,/ I shall never write another word of it,/ When along comes the Person from Porlock/ And takes the blame for it.'

Composing poems on drugs or while asleep is, with rare exceptions, an unwise thing to do. Those not yet convinced might cast an eye over 'Lysergic Acid' by Allen Ginsberg, the Laureate poems composed by Andrew Motion under the

influence of Lemsip, or the following lines, written in a
dream by Alfred, Lord Tennyson:

> **May a cock-sparrow**
> **Write to a barrow?**
> **I hope you'll excuse**
> **My infantine muse.**

* * *

If Coleridge's composition of *Kubla Khan* in a dream seems
tough, consider the unfortunate proceedings of Ibsen's trans-
lator William Archer. Archer, a theatre critic by profession,
had always been keen to prove that he had it in him to be a
playwright in his own right.

One night, a vision came to him entire just as he was
descending into sleep. He had conceived the whole plot of a
superb play from beginning to end. All that remained was to
write it down. He sank into a deep and satisfied slumber.

When he woke up, he realized that he had dreamed the
plot of *Hedda Gabler*.

* * *

At a formal dinner in Boston in 1877, Mark Twain described
the overnight stay he'd made in a mining town in Nevada.

The miner had told him, he said, that he'd been 'the
fourth literary man that has been here in twenty-four hours'
– his guests the previous night having announced themselves as Emerson ('a seedy little bit of a chap'), Holmes ('fat
as a balloon') and Longfellow ('built like a prize-fighter').
These disreputable characters had gone through their host's
beans, bacon and bourbon, and cheated him at cards. They

left early the following morning, stealing the miner's only pair of boots. 'I ain't suited to a littery atmosphere,' was the conclusion Twain's host had drawn from the encounter.

At this dinner in Boston, the story was received with great amusement, not least as 'his satirical description of the imposters was becoming regarded as an oblique satirical description of the originals'.

As Twain noted with mounting horror, though, the originals were all sitting in the audience. Not laughing. He afterwards wrote grovelling letters of apology to Holmes, Emerson and Longfellow.

This, too, backfired. Emerson wrote back saying that he couldn't understand the apology and had no memory of the speech – so Twain was then forced to make sense of it by enumerating the regretted insults, line by line, on paper for him.

* * *

The horrible demise in 1951 of the theatrical impresario Sir Charles 'Cockie' Cochran is a warning to us all. Cockie suffered terribly from arthritis, and found nothing eased the pain more than a nice hot bath. One January morning, with his wife still asleep in their bedroom at the Hyde Park Hotel, Cockie ran himself half a tub of water, climbed in, and turned off the cold tap. He then discovered that he was too stiff in the hip to reach the hot tap, which was still running.

He had, unfortunately, locked the bathroom door. Worse, just as he was reaching a rolling boil, the maid decided to run the vacuum cleaner down the corridor, drowning out his cries for help. Finally, Lady Cochran heard a wailing noise. She went to the window and looked out into the street. Nothing. Odd.

Poor old Cockie boiled to death in the bath. The fate of his rubber duck is unknown.

* * *

The publisher Christopher Sinclair-Stevenson was listening to Radio 4 one morning in 1982, and was amused by a comic play featuring a self-absorbed teenager. I must ring up the scriptwriter, he thought to himself: that could make an amusing book.

He then forgot clean about it. Until he saw, at number one in the bestseller list, and published by somebody else, *The Secret Diary of Adrian Mole, Aged 13³/₄*.

Sue Townsend was the bestselling novelist of the eighties, and the Adrian Mole books have sold more than eight million copies in thirty-four languages.

* * *

Making an amiable attempt to pass the time of day, W. S. Gilbert's barber asked him: 'When are we to expect anything further, Mr Gilbert, from your fluent pen?'

'What do you mean, sir, by "fluent pen"?' snapped the librettist. 'There is no such thing as a fluent pen. A pen is an insensible object. And, at any rate, I don't presume to pry into your private affairs; you will please observe the same reticence in regard to mine.'

The rest of the haircut passed in solemn silence.

* * *

'It's rather difficult to go on writing with so little hope of publication, but I try not to think about that,' the novelist

Barbara Pym wrote to a friend in 1974. 'By the way, the letter I wrote to *The Author* about not getting published was never published, which seems to be the final accolade of failure.'

* * *

Of the tricky business of giving a book a title, the writer Michael Frayn – who has been known to try out more than a hundred titles before finally settling on one – said that 'one of the troubles with a list of 134 titles is that it offers odds of at least 133 to one against getting it right'.

His novel *Towards the End of the Morning*, he complains, might as well be called 'The One About Fleet Street', so easily forgotten is its real name even by those who have admired it.

His low point came when, in the course of a single conversation, his own agent referred to his book *Constructions* as, variously, 'Conceptions' and 'Contractions'.

* * *

The 1927 London first night of Noël Coward's play *Sirocco* was such a fabulous disaster that its very name entered theatrical slang ('How was the show, darling?' 'Went a bit Sirocco, I'm afraid. Dicky started crying in the first scene and I had to punch him in the face.').

This dashing tale of romance tells of how a shy English holidaymaker in Italy (played by blushing starlet Frances Doble) has her inner va-va-voom awakened by a hot-blooded hunk of macho Italian man-meat – played, unfortunately, by the then campest man in show business, Ivor Novello. You might think of it as 'Shirtlift Valentine'.

The audience howled and jeered and booed. A fight broke

out in the gallery. Every time the couple had a love scene, a vocal minority of the audience interrupted it with loud and squelchy smooching noises, and when Novello appeared in his silk pyjamas and delivered the line 'I go to my mother' the house came down.

Miss Doble had, at least, one or two partisans in the crowd. 'Give the poor cow a chance!' was the gallantry that could be heard at one point over the chorus of booing. She broke character to respond, feelingly, from the stage: 'Thank you, sir. You are the only gentleman here tonight.'

The show's director – who was partially deaf – returned from supper as the play was ending. Mistaking the sound of booing for applause, and the worst flop of his career for a triumph, he instructed the curtain be raised for curtain-call after curtain-call.

When Coward himself stormed onstage to show solidarity, defiantly clasping his leading lady by the hand, someone shouted: 'Hide behind a woman, would you?'

The theatre historian Sheridan Morley describes unmatchably well what happened next, in *Theatre's Strangest Acts*:

> Now, as ice cream cartons rained down on her and the jeers increased in volume, she was in a state of hysterics, with tears pouring down her face. Mercifully resorting to auto-pilot as her spirits shrank from what was going on around her, she stuttered out, to the appalled fascination and then increased hilarity of the audience, her prepared curtain-call speech. 'Ladies and gentlemen,' she sobbed, helplessly, 'tonight is the happiest night of my life.'

* * *

The brilliant novelist Susan Hill – author of *Strange Meeting* and *The Woman in Black* – tells the following story of a brush with Hollywood.

It was 1974. I had written a novel called *In the Springtime of the Year*, loosely based on the true story of the death of my fiancé two years before, so I was unhappy and also near-bankrupt. In the early hours of one morning the phone rang. It was a man who sounded as if he had been crying. His name was Sam Goldwyn, Jr and he had been crying because he had been reading my book and somehow got my phone number, to call late at night from LA. 'I just put the book down,' he said. 'I got to the end and I had to call... to tell you that this is one of the most beautiful books I ever read in my life.'

Pause. Sob. Then came the best bit.

'Far, far too beautiful to make a movie of.'

* * *

The day after the actor Robert Morley was lavishly feted on *This Is Your Life*, his son Sheridan recounts, he ran into Rex Harrison Christmas shopping.

'Robert! I saw you on television last night,' said Harrison. 'Very impressive!' Morley, we can assume, flushed with bashful pride.

'Of course,' Harrison continued, 'I, with so many wives... so many divorces, couldn't possibly do *This Is Your Life*. But you, Robert – you've had such a different life. I mean, one wife, one family, one house... and, of course, one performance. Happy Christmas!'

* * *

The curse on Shakespeare's Scottish Play – as we are all obliged to call it – is a story all of its own.

In 1606, Shakespeare had to play Lady Macbeth himself, when the boy actor due to take the role keeled over and died. In 1672, a mix-up with daggers saw the lead in an Amsterdam production stab Duncan to death on stage in front of a live audience. In a 1721 production the actors left the stage to attack a hostile audience with their swords, and the army was called in. In 1849, a performance in New York degenerated into a riot in which thirty-one people were trampled.

In a 1937 production, Lady Macduff and the director were involved in a car crash on the way to the theatre, and the proprietor of the theatre expired during the dress rehearsal. A 25 lb weight crashed out of the flies and narrowly avoided killing Laurence Olivier; less lucky was the man in the audience struck by Olivier's sword when it broke and flew off the stage, who later suffered a heart attack. The year 1934 saw a Macbeth struck dumb on stage, and his two replacements hospitalized one after the other.

A 1942 production saw three deaths and two suicides among the cast and crew. In 1947 an actor was stabbed to death in a swordfight. In 1953, Charlton Heston's tights caught fire. A 1971 production suffered two fires and seven muggings.

When Peter O'Toole and Frances Tomelty played the Macbeths in 1980, the curse was on ripping form. Tomelty came off her motorbike at 70 mph, O'Toole was involved in a car accident, and First Witch suffered a burst appendix. Having battled through all this adversity, they were greeted by hysterical laughter from the audience. One reviewer judged the show 'not so much downright bad as heroically ludicrous'.

* * *

At a 1986 London preview performance of Andrew Lloyd-Webber's unimaginably successful musical *The Phantom of the Opera* – now the longest-running Broadway musical in history – Sod descended gleefully on the cast.

This was a show that, it must be said, asks for trouble. Each performance uses 230 costumes, 120 automated cues, 22 scene changes, 281 candles and 250 kg of dry ice. There are ten smoke machines and, during the course of the show, a one-ton chandelier has to drop out of the sky. The touring production travels round in twenty-seven pantechnicons.

During the tempestuous climax in the Phantom's lair, on this occasion, all the electricals decided to malfunction at once. The Phantom's spooky pipe-organ had slid in from the wings, and those 281 candles, as planned, rose up through the floor of the stage and started flickering romantically. Then, just as the Phantom whirled his paramour across the stage, every single trapdoor flopped open as if in an Indiana Jones film.

Mysteriously, the pipe-organ retreated from the stage, and wandering back on stage came Sarah Brightman's bed, which had played a pivotal part in the previous scene.

Singing gamely on, Michael Crawford – no doubt now suffering a *Some Mothers Do 'Ave 'Em* flashback – picked his way between the abyssal pitfalls and contrived to ignore the bed.

Down crashed a giant portcullis from still another scene. And rather than staying put, those 281 candles started sinking into the floor and shooting up again at random – one of them sliding neatly up Crawford's trouser-leg, pinning him to the spot and agonizingly burning his bare shin.

Still, on he warbled, trouper to the last.

SODDING POLITICS, SODDING POLITICIANS, AND SODDING PUBLIC LIFE

The former American president Richard Milhous Nixon takes a distinguished place in the annals of Sod's Law.

Not only did he tempt fate beyond the limits of endurance by publicly declaring 'I am not a crook' – which is, as his successor Bill 'I did not have sexual relations with that woman' Clinton was to discover, a standing invitation to the universe to prove you wrong. The fact that he made this declaration at Disneyworld was a red rag to a bull.

He also, with a thoroughness that his deadliest political opponent could not have hoped to match, gathered the evidence that would expose him. The problem was that though Nixon was by all accounts a clever fellow, he was also bug-eyed with paranoia.

He drew up lists of people he thought were out to get him. People out to get Nixon, from where he was sitting, looked like a broad church: 'liberals, Democrats, intellectuals, journalists, and the Eastern establishment elite'. And singers, actors, chemists... you name it.

His 'Opponents List' and 'Political Enemies Project' – to pals, just 'Enemies List' – included Teddy Kennedy, the *New York Times*, the *Washington Post* (prescient, that one), Barbra

Streisand, and Carl Djerassi, inventor of the contraceptive pill. Oh, and Bill Cosby.

A memorandum from Nixon's White House counsel John Dean explained in his characteristically nuanced legalese that the purpose of the list was to 'use the available federal machinery to screw our political enemies'.

The federal machinery, of course, ended up screwing Nixon like a man who catches his tie in an industrial mangle – but so did machinery of another sort.

For another manifestation of Nixon's paranoia was the insistence on installing secret voice-activated tape recorders in the Oval Office to record everything that was said. If you're going to participate in a highly illegal cover-up, recording yourself doing it isn't too smart.

When the acronymically unfortunate Committee to Re-Elect the President (CREEP) was fingered for its involvement in burgling the Democratic National Committee headquarters in the Watergate Hotel, President Nixon ordered the CIA to halt its investigation in the interests of national security.

That, unfortunately, didn't put an end to the story. But he still might have got away with it had it not been for a spectacular courtroom boo-boo by a senior aide.

At one point Mr Dean – he of the 'screw our enemies' memo – mentioned something to the special Senate committee that implied some of his conversations with the President might have been taped.

The Watergate Committee asked a senior Nixon box-wallah, Alexander Butterfield, whether there were recording devices in the Oval Office and whether therefore Mr Dean might have been taped.

Instead of just saying, as might have been sensible, 'Yes', Mr Butterfield went a bit further. With the immortal words, 'I was hoping you fellows wouldn't ask me about that,' he announced: 'Well... yes, a recording system [was] in the president's office.'

Then he added: 'Everything was taped. As long as the President was in attendance. There was not so much as a hint that something should not be taped.'

Can over, worms everywhere.

There existed a minute-by-minute archive of everything the President had ever said to anybody in the Oval Office. Before Mr Butterfingers's unhelpful intervention, they had no idea such a thing existed.

It was the matter of a moment to subpoena the tapes – and the matter of a few months (and some vicious but ultimately futile sackings in the Justice Department) to have the Supreme Court overturn Nixon's claim they were protected by executive privilege.

Eventually, he coughed them up. On 29 April 1974, he told the public that what he was handing over would 'include all the relevant portions of all the subpoenaed conversations that were recorded, that is, all portions that relate to the question of what I knew about Watergate or the cover-up and what I did about it.'

Was he off the hook? Sod again intervened again in the form of some sharp-eyed technicians, who noticed that eighteen minutes of conversation had been deliberately excised from the tapes.

After a few more weeks of insisting that the dog had eaten his homework, the most powerful man on earth was forced to hand over the missing bits. They confirmed that he'd been covering up CREEP's illegal activities since 1972. His misfeasances were regarded as bad enough in those days to secure him an interview with David Frost.

* * *

In 1977, the United States Department of Agriculture named its new cafeteria in Washington – the Alfred Packer Memorial Dining Facility – in honour of the rough-hewn nineteenth-century Colorado frontiersman.

'Alfred Packer,' declared US Agriculture Secretary Robert Bergland as he unveiled a brass plaque, 'exemplifies the spirit and fare that this agriculture department cafeteria will provide.'

A few months later, the General Services Administration removed the dedicatory plaque, and renamed the cafeteria. It emerged that Packer had been hanged in 1874 for killing and eating five prospectors who had hired him to guide them along the Mormon Trail into Colorado.

* * *

The distinguished German architect Helmut Jahn's first major project was the construction of the multi-million-dollar Kemper Arena in Kansas City, Missouri. In recognition of the young architect's achievement, he was presented in 1976 with an award for the building from the American Institute of Architects. Thousands of the Institute's members returned to the building in 1979 for their annual conference. Less than twenty-four hours later, the roof collapsed.

* * *

Early on in my researches for this book, I found myself at a party for the excellent tri-quarterly magazine *Areté* (subscription enquiries: 8 New College Lane, Oxford, OX1 3BN). There, I fell into conversation about my project with Deborah, a young editor on the *London Review of Books*.

The *LRB* is a left-leaning literary journal, the general consensus among whose contributors is that Israel is more sinning than sinned against. Considerably more sinning. At the time, the *LRB*'s corporate hostility to Israel was so fierce, in fact, that Deborah – American by birth – was probably the only person in the office who didn't feel that the *LRB*'s advocacy of an Apartheid-era-South-Africa-style trade boycott of Israel was appropriate. She found herself overcome with pity for the innocent Israeli artisans and farmers who would be the victims of such an embargo.

'I decided to make a statement,' she told me. She had gone out to the shop and bought a box of Israeli dates. These, she had brought ostentatiously back into the office, her head held high. She may even have offered them around.

Amid an atmosphere of trembling disapproval, she removed a juicy date from the box, bit into it – and broke her tooth on the stone. The *LRB*'s editor, Mary-Kay Wilmers, generously passed on the details of her dentist.

* * *

Sod's Law occasionally works against itself. That is, if everybody becomes utterly convinced that something is going to go wrong – and takes massive and expensive precautions against it doing so – it can be more or less guaranteed to go right; and to go right in such a way as to make clear that all those precautions were a complete waste of time.

There are few better instances of this than the Millennium Bug. As the year 2000 approached, some people noticed something and started to fret. For most of the years people had been making computers, they had used two digits in their date counters. So the dates were counting up in sequence: 95, 96, 97 and so on. What would happen, they wondered, when at the stroke of midnight on 31 December 1999, billions of date counters in billions of computers across the world flipped over from 99 to 00?

Aeroplanes would fall from the sky, phone networks would crash, stock markets would vanish, the sky would be dark with accidentally launched nuclear warheads, and a rider on a pale horse would interrupt the New Year's Eve celebrations in Sydney to announce the end of the world.

Government agencies were established to combat the problem, companies sprang up offering Y2K insurance and Y2K legal representation and packets of tinned goods for survivalists. The BBC estimated that measures to combat the bug had cost £300 billion worldwide.

The bug – in the event – caused no major problems anywhere at all. Indeed, a senior Slovenian Y2K official was given the sack by his peevish paymasters for scaremongering.

In Rayong, Thailand, grilled-squid saleswoman Kieuthong Attapharb withdrew her life savings of £1,650 from the bank for fear that they would be wiped out by the Millennium Bug. On 2 January – two days before she was proposing to put the money back in the bank – her house burned down and she lost the lot.

* * *

The field of political assassination is one in which Sod has long taken a very particular interest. The Stauffenberg plot to kill Hitler failed, as every schoolboy knows, because the briefcase containing the bomb was on the other side of a heavy table leg from the Führer. In the event, it only blew his trousers off, lending an unwelcome comic-opera tinge to what was supposed to be a turning point in the history of the world.

Killing off the priapic Russian quack Grigori Rasputin, though, made disposing of the Führer seem like a walk in the park. 'The soul of this wretched peasant seems to have been sewn onto his body' was the judgement of one observer. They were not wrong.

First up was Khionia Gusyeva – a crazed prostitute with no nose who was a disciple of a rival monk. She ambushed him after church and knifed him in the guts. 'I have killed the Antichrist!' she shrieked. She spoke way too soon. Rasputin lumbered off down the street with his entrails hanging out, and she chased after him in the hopes of finishing the job. He bopped her on the head with a bit of wood, and she was carted off to the loony bin. Rasputin one; death nil.

Rasputin had many enemies – as you might expect for a man who became to the Romanov royals what Sir Laurens Van der Post was to the young Prince Charles. What finally did for him was a conspiracy headed by Prince Felix Yusupov, to whose house in St Petersburg he was lured.

They served the bearded wonder some cakes and wine, both dosed with enough cyanide to kill several normal men. He scoffed the lot without any appearance of being affected. 'The monk was even merrier than before,' reported Colonel Stanislaus de Lazovert later. Getting twitchy, the conspirators turned to Plan B. Yusupov shot him in the back. He fell over.

Job done, they thought. They were just heading off when Yusupov decided to pop back to get his coat. At which point Rasputin's supposed corpse leapt to its feet and started to strangle him with the (near-literally) immortal words: 'You bad boy!'

Yusupov wrestled free and ran to get the others, while Rasputin decided to take to his own toes. The conspirators returned, shot him three times in the back, stabbed him and beaned him for good measure. Then they tied him to a chair and threw him into the freezing river.

The autopsy concluded that what actually killed him

was not poison, cold, stabbing or blunt force trauma but drowning.

In 2004, evidence emerged to suggest that Rasputin had, in fact, simply been shot in the head by the British Secret Service. But that's what they would want you to think, isn't it?

* * *

The undisputed champion of Sod's Law working to your advantage in the field of assassination, though, is (at the time of writing) alive and well and living in Cuba.

The CIA has been trying to kill Fidel Castro for half a century, and has yet to harm so much as a hair on his godless communist head. The book I have on the subject, *CIA Targets Fidel*, was bought from a thriving Cuban holiday resort. It is proudly offered for sale throughout the island and appears to be a modest bestseller. It is a reprint of a recently declassified 1967 CIA document, and it describes an epic balls-up from murderous start to harmless finish.

The contents page hints at the cornucopia of wizard wheezes within. The pre-1960 section contains 'Aerosol Attack on Radio Station', 'Contaminated Cigars' and, mysteriously, 'Depilatory'. Before 1960, they were prepared to settle for character assassination. These first two schemes were plans to introduce LSD into, respectively, Castro's radio station and his cigars in the hopes of making his speeches embarrassingly silly. The third scheme was a proposal to dust Castro's shoes with thallium salts on an overseas visit in the hopes of making his beard fall out.

That got nowhere.

Encouraged by the galloping successes of these plots, the CIA decided after 1960 to go one better and kill him off altogether. They decided, at first, that the best way to do this was to get in cahoots with Cuba-connected figures from the criminal underworld such as Sam Giancana – whose involvement, embarrassingly, became public after a botched wiretapping operation.

That got nowhere.

They had a go at persuading the Cubans to bump him off themselves, bombarding the coastline with floating carrier bags containing bribes of chewing gum and propaganda leaflets offering a $150,000 bounty for killing Fidel (Che Guevara was a disappointing $120,000).

That got nowhere.

Methods the CIA subsequently investigated included dropping poisoned pills into his drink ('failed to dissolve'), 'lethal cigars', bacterial warfare by handkerchief, shellfish poison administered with a pin, a ballpoint pen converted into a hypodermic syringe, and – in desperation – the dull old last resort: 'high-powered rifle with telescopic sight'.

The high-water mark of their inventiveness, though, centred around Fidel's known fondness for snorkelling. In early 1963 – shortly after their attempt to sponsor a wholesale invasion of the island had gone a bit wrong at the Bay of Pigs (a coastal inlet whose name is now indelibly linked with the word 'fiasco') – a plan was devised to present Castro with a skin-diving suit. But not just any skin-diving suit: this one would have its inside surface dusted with a fungus that would give him an incurable and unsightly disease called 'Madura foot'.

This plan was abandoned as 'obviously impracticable'. So, the pragmatists back at the CIA hit on what appears in the report as 'Booby-trapped Sea Shell'. They intended, in all seriousness, 'to take an unusually spectacular sea shell that would be certain to catch Castro's eye, load it with an explosive triggered to blow when the shell was lifted, and submerge it in an area where Castro often went skin-diving'.

Their agent even went so far as to buy two books on Caribbean Mollusca – and there he hit his hitch: 'None of the shells that might conceivably be found in the Caribbean area was both spectacular enough to be sure of attracting attention and large enough to hold the needed volume of explosive. The midget submarine,' the report adds, which is surely painting the lily, 'that would have had to be used in emplacement of the shell has too short an operating range for such an operation.'

None of these plans, not one, got anywhere. It looks overwhelmingly likely that Fidel Castro will die of old age.

Good job all round, the Central Intelligence Agency.

This is the same CIA, incidentally, which in 1950 predicted that the Chinese wouldn't dare invade Korea (two days later, they did); which in 1962 was taken completely by surprise when it emerged that there were Soviet nuclear missiles next door in Cuba; which failed to learn that Mikhail Gorbachev had promised not to invade Eastern Europe; was dumbfounded by the withdrawal of the Red Army from Afghanistan; failed entirely to predict the collapse of the Soviet Union; had not a single Farsi-speaking agent after the Iranian revolution; and in 1990, with Iraqi troops massing on the border with Kuwait, confidently assured the President that Saddam was 'bluffing'.

* * *

What mother has not, at some time or another, heard to the fortissimo accompaniment of slamming doors, the age-old cry of 'Mum! I HATE you! You won't let me do ANYTHING!'?

As it is now, so it was in the ancient world – witness the Emperor Nero's fraught relationship with his mother

Agrippina. She scolded him about his girlfriend, poked her nose into the affairs of state, and made a general nuisance of herself – even agitating at one point for Nero's 15-year-old kid brother to be put in charge.

Initially, according to Suetonius's *Lives of the Twelve Caesars*, he simply sulked: 'His mother being used to make strict inquiry into what he said or did, and to reprimand him with the freedom of a parent, he was so much offended, that he endeavoured to expose her to public resentment, by frequently pretending a resolution to quit the government, and retire to Rhodes.'

Then he took more drastic measures to shut the old bag up. 'Soon afterwards, he deprived her of all honour and power, took from her the guard of Roman and German soldiers, banished her from the palace and from his society, and persecuted her in every way he could contrive; employing persons to harass her when at Rome with law-suits, and to disturb her in her retirement from town with the most scurrilous and abusive language, following her about by land and sea.'

Finally, he decided the only solution was to bump her off. Here, the Sod truly enters the picture. Three times he tried to poison her. She saw that coming, though, and 'had previously secured herself by antidotes'.

Next, he tried the old collapsing ceiling ruse: 'he contrived machinery, by which the floor over her bed-chamber might be made to fall upon her while she was asleep in the night'. That didn't work either. Somebody blabbed and she switched bedrooms.

Next came the falling-apart ship scheme. He had his engineers construct a ship specially designed to fall apart like a Buster Keaton stage set when subjected to the slightest knock. His idea was that the old bag would catch it either when the deck collapsed into her cabin, or by drowning when the ship went to the bottom.

Then under cover of a pretend reconciliation, he wrote her an affectionate letter. Why didn't she let bygones be bygones, and come over to Baiae to celebrate the festival of Minerva with him.

He then had a word with the captains of the escort ships. They were to accidentally bump into Agrippina's special collapsey deathtrap ship on the way back. Job, he thought, done.

They had a blast at the festival, which Nero prolonged so as to ensure Mumsy would be making her return journey by night. In a mood of uncommon cheerfulness, according to Suetonius, Nero kissed his mother's breasts (a gesture of filial piety, apparently) and waved her off at the harbour.

Then he 'sat up very late in the night, waiting with great anxiety to learn the issue of his project'.

The issue of his project was, unfortunately, that Agrippina was wet, cross, and very much alive. Turned out she knew how to swim.

This news of her survival was brought to Nero by Agrippina's servant Lucius Agerinus, 'bringing word, with great joy, that she was safe and well'. Here, the forces of embuggerance turned on Lucius.

Nero decided on the spot to adopt a direct approach. He dropped a dagger at Lucius's feet, shouted words to the effect of 'Help! Murder! My mother's slave just tried to kill me!' and demanded that the guards seize him.

He swiftly had his mother done in, and put it about that she'd committed suicide.

* * *

John Major's 1993 declaration that his Conservative government needed to go 'Back to Basics' was an open invitation to the forces of embuggerment (in some cases quite literally). It may rank as the least successful moral rearmament campaign ever.

Over the next few years, his married environment minister Tim Yeo fathered a bastard child with a Tory councillor; a junior whip, Michael Brown, was 'outed' having a relationship with an underage man; a married backbencher, David Ashby, was caught sharing a bed with another chap; another Tory MP, Hartley Booth, resigned after falling in love with his parliamentary researcher; another MP, Stephen Milligan, was found dead of auto-erotic asphyxia with an orange in his mouth and ladies' stockings on his legs; another MP, Piers Merchant, was caught sleeping with a nightclub hostess; a whole raft of Tory MPs were found to have been accepting bribes from Mohamed al-Fayed; and Major's Chief Secretary to the Treasury, Jonathan Aitken, declared his intention 'to cut out the cancer of bent and twisted journalism in our country with the simple sword of truth and the trusty shield of British fair play' – a fight that collapsed just as he was on the point of suborning his teenage daughter to lie for him under oath.

At least, Major could console himself, the libellous suggestion that he had been having an extra-marital affair with the Downing Street cook had been seen off in court. He had actually, it emerged later, been having an extra-marital affair with Edwina Currie.

* * *

Chris Cleave's first novel, *Incendiary*, was framed as a letter to Osama bin Laden written by a woman who lost her child in a terrorist attack on London. The launch party was scheduled for 7 July 2005. It was cancelled.

* * *

In the late 1890s, the Abyssinian Emperor Menelik II learned that a new method of judicial execution was catching on in the West: the electric chair. Determined that Abyssinia should be at the cutting edge of capital punishment, he ordered three. Abyssinia did not, at the time, have any means of generating electricity. He used one of the chairs as a throne.

* * *

In 1939, King George VI and Queen Elizabeth were touring Canada. When they arrived in Winnipeg, they were greeted by the Canadian Prime Minister Mackenzie King, and the Mayor of Winnipeg, John Queen, and his wife.

The live broadcast of the event on Canadian radio sounded as follows:

Here comes the Royal Family now. The automobile has now stopped...

Oh, there's the King – he's stepping out, followed by Her Majesty Queen Elizabeth, nattily attired in a silver coat.

Mr King is now shaking hands with the King and introducing Mr Queen to the King and Queen and then Mrs Queen to the Queen and King.

They are now proceeding up the steps to the well-decorated City Hall, the King and Mr King together with the Queen being escorted by Mrs Queen. The King has now stopped and said something to Mr Queen and Mrs Queen and the Queen and Mr King and the Queen laughed jovially. The King leaves Mr King and goes to Mrs Queen, and Mr Queen and Mr King follow behind...

* * *

In 1944, Winston Churchill summoned the political philosopher Isaiah Berlin to lunch. Berlin was at that time playing an important role in the war effort, reporting from the British Embassy in Washington on American public opinion. Churchill wanted to pick his brains.

'So, Mr Berlin,' said Churchill as lunch finished. 'What's the most important piece of work you have done for us lately?'

Churchill was disconcerted when the answer came: 'It would be "White Christmas", I guess.'

Nevertheless, he persevered: 'Now tell me, what in your opinion is the likelihood of my dear friend, the President, being re-elected for a fourth term?'

Berlin responded that he thought Roosevelt was indeed popular enough to clinch it, but that if he failed to stand as a candidate, he didn't think he'd bother to vote at all. Churchill, who hadn't been aware that Isaiah Berlin would even have a vote in the American elections, was again flummoxed.

He asked a third question. 'When do you think the European War is going to end?' At which point Berlin looked overcome with pride.

'Sir,' Berlin responded in a voice choked with emotion, 'I shall never forget this moment. When I go back to my own country I shall tell my children and my children's children that in the spring of 1944 the Prime Minister of Great Britain asked *me* when the European War was going to end.'

They parted company, Churchill baffled that the distinguished professor had turned out to be such a blithering idiot. Irving Berlin – the American popular songwriter of the same name whom Churchill had invited to lunch in error – was equally confused. He returned to his hotel room at the Savoy and reported to a friend that though Churchill was undoubtedly a great man, 'I somehow felt we didn't click'.

THE QUEST FOR
KNOWLEDGE

Lake Peigneur was a pretty, ten-foot-deep freshwater lake in Louisiana popular with fishermen from the surrounding area. A small island on the lake was given over to a botanical garden, and the area was rich in natural mineral resources: deep underneath it were miles of tunnels belonging to the Diamond Crystal salt mine, and across the surrounding landscape were dotted richly productive oil wells.

Early one November morning in 1980, twelve employees of Texaco Petroleum, aboard an oil rig in the middle of the lake, were drilling an exploratory hole when their drilling rig suddenly seized up, more than 1,000 feet below the surface.

Try as they might, they couldn't seem to free it. Suddenly, there came a series of ominous plops and belches from the muddy depths, and the rig listed over alarmingly. The oilmen weren't sure what was going to happen, but decided that the safest place to watch it from was the shore.

As they reached shore, behind them the $5 million rig turned turtle and vanished beneath the surface of the lake – a lake that was supposed to be only ten feet deep. Moments later, where the rig had been, the water started to turn. A whirlpool formed.

Texaco, as it turned out, had miscalculated the position of the Diamond Crystal salt mine, and drilled a fourteen-inch hole in the top of one of the main shafts. The water rushed into the salt dome, dissolving the salt and steadily enlarging the hole as it went.

As if the plug had been pulled out of a ten-square-mile bathtub – the entire contents of the lake started to disappear into the mines.

As miners scrambled to evacuate the salt mines and the oilmen watched the carnage, gobsmacked, from the shore, one local fisherman steered his boat to shore, tied it to a tree and leaped out – only to watch boat and tree both vanish into the whirlpool. Pockets of compressed air in the salt-mines exploded into 400-foot geysers.

The whirlpool also swallowed another drilling platform, a barge loading dock, five houses, seventy acres of soil from Jefferson Island, most of the botanical gardens, trucks, trees, a motor home and a parking lot. So powerful was the suction that it reversed the flow of a canal leading from the lake to the Gulf of Mexico, creating a 164-foot waterfall (the tallest – temporarily – in the state of Louisiana) and sucking eleven barges and a manned tugboat into the salt mines.

Two days later, nine of the barges popped back up to the surface like corks.

Nobody was hurt.

* * *

Edgar Allan Poe, immodest though he was, would have been startled to open the ninth edition of the *Encyclopaedia Britannica* and discover himself cited as an authority on 'whirlpools'. A dozy encyclopaedist credited Poe for information that he had copied directly out of a previous edition of *Britannica*, and repeated the poet's own invented embellishments as fact. *Britannica*'s entry on 'Edgar Allan Poe' is more reliable.

* * *

Sod's Law accounts for the only time I've been successfully sued for libel. In the late nineties I was working as the deputy editor of a diary column on the *Daily Mail*. One day, my then boss took it into his head to compose a somewhat controversial paragraph about a Republican-supporting Irish journalist named Eamonn McCann.

As was the custom, I ran to the newspaper's library to fetch the envelope of press cuttings about Mr McCann, and riffled through it for background material. Three or four of the cuttings in the envelope made reference to a 1970s conviction for manslaughter, which I mentioned to the boss.

His eventual item, which was risky enough in itself if you ask me, made reference to the 'combustible Mr McCann', adding the parenthesis that he was 'once jailed for manslaughter'.

The following day, when Mr McCann's writ arrived, I went back to the library in a panic and called up the cuttings on Eamonn McCann. I riffled through them in search of the ones relating to the conviction. They had vanished.

When I mentioned this, in a panic, to the librarian, he asked: 'Oh – you mean the *other* Eamonn McCann!' And he fetched a brown envelope, marked 'Eamonn McCann' in ink still wet enough to come off on my fingers, and containing four cuttings that looked distinctly familiar, relating to the manslaughter conviction of a man who happened to have exactly the same name as our blameless brother journalist.

The mistake cost the *Daily Mail* more than my annual salary.

* * *

<frank>: can you help me install GTA3?
<knightmare>: first, shut down all programs you aren't using
frank has quit IRC. (Quit)
<knightmare>:...

(Fragmentary transcript from an Internet chat room,
archived at www.bash.org)

* * *

In the matter of friendship, there are those who have the gift, and those who do not. The philosopher James Mill was of the latter camp. A new recruit to the East India Company, where he worked, asked his colleague Thomas Love Peacock: 'When I know Mill well, shall I like him – will he like what I like and hate what I hate?' Peacock thought for a minute. 'No,' he said. 'He will hate what you hate, and hate everything you like.'

* * *

Nasa's *Mariner 1* space probe was, in the early sixties, the boldest and most distant space exploration yet conceived. This probe was to travel all the way to Venus, a journey that would take nearly four months at speeds of 25,280 mph. There, it would pass over the surface of the planet and beam back data about the gases that surround it.

It launched from Cape Canaveral on 22 July 1962 in a magnificent cloud of flame, sailed into the clear skies – and then took a sharp and unplanned turn to the north-east, advertising a strong likelihood of it ploughing either into the crowded North Atlantic shipping lanes or an inhabited area on land.

The range's safety officer – after the spaceship had been in the air only 293 seconds – pressed the panic button and the spacecraft exploded prettily in mid-air.

Mariner's five-minute flight – which took it nowhere near Venus – cost Nasa, according to the *New York Times*, $18,500,000. The failure of its guidance system was attributed to a 'missing hyphen' in the software.

* * *

Mariner 1, of course, was only one of a whole series of superb cock-ups in the history of space exploration. (An old story concerns a young lad in class being asked to count to ten. He says: 'Ten, nine, eight, seven, six, five, four, three, SHIT!' It emerges that his father works for Nasa.)

In the early afternoon of 11 December 1998, the *Mars Climate Orbiter* lifted into the air from its Cape Canaveral launch pad and sailed out of our atmosphere on a mission to the planet that has baffled and fascinated men more than any other.

The craft was to enter orbit just under 100 miles above the surface of the mysterious red planet, where it would sit and observe the weather systems that swept scouring clouds of red dust across the Martian surface. It would search for evidence that the barren planet's climate had once been different – for water vapour in the atmosphere, for a hint, perhaps, that those canals and craters had, millions of years ago, been the cradle of unknown life.

That was the idea, anyway.

All went well at first. On Boxing Day, a brief blast on the thrusters was used to correct the orbit. On 23 September the following year, the Orbiter reached Mars. The engines were ignited to insert it into its orbit, and just after nine in the morning it passed behind the red planet. If all went to plan, it would re-emerge on the other side ten minutes or so later and, so to speak, wave hello to earth. The scientists waited.

Ten minutes passed. They continued to wait.

They never heard from it again. The reason? The thrusters on the spaceship that were intended to control its rate of rotation had been accidentally programmed in imperial, rather than metric measurements.

The thrusters were giving between four and five times less oomph than they were meant to, and so instead of passing a safe 100 miles above the Martian surface, the Orbiter went in at about a height of 30 miles, and friction from the Martian atmosphere burned it to a frazzle.

The total cost of sending what was, effectively, a firework to Mars was $327,600,000. Or, in imperial measures, that's roughly 253,000,000 pounds.

* * *

In 1990, Penguin published their *Spelling Dictionary*, which boasted of being 'the clearest, most extensive spelling dictionary now available'.

'From aa, Aachen and aardvaak,' the back cover boasted, 'to wowser and yoicks, zymase and Zyrian, over 70,000 headwords give all the spellings most people will need.'

'Aardvaak' should actually read 'aardvark', as its entry on page one inside confirms.

* * *

The failure of the *Mars Climate Orbiter* was, even Nasa would have had to admit, something of a setback. Hope, however, sprang eternal. Hard on its interplanetary heels came the second part of their project: the *Mars Polar Lander*.

This was to touch the very surface of the red planet –

alighting on the barren wastes of southern Mars a few hundred miles from the pole, near the edge of the vast carbon-dioxide ice-cap that blankets the pole in the chilly Martian springtime. There, it would sit and observe the weather systems that swept scouring clouds of blah blah blah across the Martian surface. It had cameras, gas analysers, and even a miniature microphone to record what Mars sounds like.

It would search for evidence that the barren planet's climate had once been different – for water vapour in the atmosphere or crystals of ice in the soil: for a hint, perhaps, that those canals and craters had, millions of years ago, been the cradle of unknown life.

You can see where this is going, can't you?

Long story short, it took off fine, hurtled off through space and arrived in the rough area of Mars two and a half months behind its doomed little buddy the *Orbiter*. On 3 December 1999, it sent the electronic equivalent of a big hello to ground control, descended into the atmosphere – and was never heard from again.

Nasa's best guess as to what happened is that, as it was descending through the atmosphere, atmospheric turbulence caused its legs to vibrate. The on-board computer mistook those wobbles for the jolt of contact with land – and so turned the thrusters off 40 yards above the Martian surface. Leaving the *Lander* to touch down with all the grace and elegance of an air-conditioning unit thrown out of an apartment window.

* * *

No account of the history of Martian exploration, of course, should be without mention of battling Brit Professor

Colin Pillinger: scientist, dreamer, turkey farmer*. A man who, one would like to think, would programme all his spaceships in imperial measures just to defy meddling EU bureaucrats.

Unlike Nasa, which as we've seen throws hundreds of millions of dollars at its failures, the *Mars Express* mission was run on a shoestring. The whole thing cost between £60 million and £70 million.

Still, the objective was about the same as Nasa's. Sit on the surface of Mars, yadda yadda, scouring dusty winds, yadda yadda, ancient and mysterious yadda yadda search for evidence yadda crystals of ice yadda yadda cradle of unknown life. Oh, and it was proposing a panoramic happy-snap of the planet's surface: the sort of image that, if all went well, would be a fixture on every schoolboy's bedroom wall by the following year.

The *Mars Express* mothership – launched from a Kazakh cosmodrome on 2 June 2003 – was to make its way to Mars. There, it would enter orbit and dispatch *Beagle 2* in the general direction of the planet's surface. None of your silly retro-rockets this time. *Beagle 2* was equipped with good old-fashioned parachutes and a sort of driver's-side airbag arrangement to cushion its landing.

It was due to make landfall on 25 December. Anyway, long story – once again – short, the tangerine in Professor Pillinger's Christmas stocking tasted less sweet that year.

Nobody knows what happened to *Beagle 2*. Did its parachutes fail to open and it go splat into the surface of Mars? Did it miss Mars altogether and shoot off into the sun? Or did it, as I prefer to believe, land safely, discover the evidence for life on Mars, and then decide to keep its own counsel?

Only *Beagle 2* knows, and it's not telling.

*according to Wikipedia, though I have my doubts about this detail

* * *

On 1 January 2004, the *Daily Telegraph* published a coloratura eyewitness report of the previous night's Hogmanay celebrations in Edinburgh – the crowds of thousands of revellers; the spectacular firework display; the skirl of bagpipes and the infectious feeling of celebration.

It was vivid, but inaccurate in one significant particular. Edinburgh's New Year's Eve celebrations in 2003 were cancelled owing to driving rain and hurricane-force winds.

If you look at the newspaper's electronic archive these days, the report has disappeared. In its place appears a peevish article headlined 'Edinburgh Defends Hogmany [*sic*] Party Cancellation'.

* * *

Scholars differ on the matter of the most inadvertently pathetic newspaper front page ever. My vote goes to a particular front-page splash in the *Sunday Mirror* in the late nineties.

The paper had what it thought was quite a scoop on its hands: a grainy paparazzi shot of the veteran lady-seducer, singer and wrinkle-collector Rod Stewart emerging from a nightclub with an attractive blonde lady who was not his wife.

In the absence of any proper news, this was one to go big on. The paper cleared the front page, and filled it with this photograph and this photograph alone. The identity of Rod's lady friend being, as yet, unknown, the headline – in 72-point block capitals – asked: 'WHO'S THE MYSTERY BLONDE WITH ROD STEWART?'

It was only as the presses were about to roll that the newspaper discovered that the man in the picture was not Rod

Stewart at all, but a member of the public with a similar hair-style.

It was too late to redesign the page. The following morning, readers of the *Sunday Mirror* were greeted by the hard-hitting headline: 'WHO'S THE MYSTERY BLONDE WITH THE MYSTERY BLOND?'

* * *

When Stephen Pile's *The Book of Heroic Failures* – a pioneering work in the study of Sod's Law, and a huge UK bestseller – was published in the United States, it flopped.

'Sales took ages to reach double figures,' Pile wrote with approval in his introduction to its 1988 sequel, adding:

> Furthermore, readers will be glad to hear that the American edition came out with an erratum slip which was longer than the one listed in the book as a world record. (They omitted a healthy chunk of the introduction, an improvement which added a much-needed air of mystery to the work.)
>
> When the Taiwan pirate edition came out, they knew nothing of this erratum slip with the result that their excellent version began 'And so in 1976' .

* * *

Ever since Prometheus stole fire from the gods (and look where that got him – strapped to a rock while an overgrown pigeon chews his liver for all eternity), man has striven to lay bare the secrets of the universe.

Perhaps the pinnacle of our species' practical attempts to get to the bottom of What It's All About has been the construction of the Large Hadron Collider at Cern. Getting on for £5 billion has been spent on constructing this colossal boondoggle, which will beam subatomic particles at unimaginable speeds around a seventeen-mile, doughnut-shaped tunnel underneath the Swiss-French border.

According to scientists – or 'boffins', as the popular press prefers to call them – the collisions between these particles have the potential to recreate the conditions of the very beginning of the universe, test some of the most advanced assumptions of particle physics, and coax the shy and elusive 'Higgs boson' out of its shell and on to the dance floor.

According to the popular press, and several concerned citizens – some of them brandishing writs – the collisions between these particles also had the potential to create 'strangelets', spew antimatter, and bring about a microscopic black hole that would pull the universe inside out through its own arsehole.

In the event, neither thing happened. On 10 September 2008 the big electric doughnut was turned on (to the disappointment of the popular press, who had asked for a red button or, ideally, a plunger, this turned out not to be a very telegenic event) and almost immediately broke, an event which was even less telegenic.

It's now expected to start working again at around the end of September 2009 – which is two months before the volume you hold in your hands was supposed to be flying from the front tables of bookshops and into the Christmas stockings of unloved distant relatives up and down the country.

Are you reading these words? If so, the Large Hadron Collider has not brought the world to an end, and I can expect a royalty cheque. Sweet.

* * *

The late editor and columnist John Junor had the lifelong, and wholly baseless, conviction that nobody could be sued for simply asking a question.

The phrase 'Richard Whiteley is a murderous pederast', he would have argued, was a costly libel action waiting to happen. You were as safe as houses, on the other hand, writing: 'I do not claim to know whether or not Richard Whiteley is a murderous pederast. But don't you think the public has a right to know?'

This demented article of faith was the ruination of many of the great man's less fortunate disciples. He, naturally, soldiered on unscathed – except for once.

A certain schoolteacher had just been exonerated, for the third time in a row, of interfering with young boys. J. J. wrote a column in which he congratulated the man archly on his acquittal, but mused that in future perhaps he'd be well advised to take up a line of work 'that carries a less high risk of false accusation'.

So pleased was J. J. with this *bon mot* that he included it in *The Best of JJ*, the book-length collection of his columnar greatest hits. At which point the man in question – having not seen the original item – sued, causing the entire run of the book to have to be pulped.

* * *

Legend tells us of a misguided old woman who swallowed a fly. Irritated by the low-level gastric buzzing of the insect – which, so the story goes, wriggled and jiggled and tickled inside her – this woman went on to swallow whole a spider, a bird, a cat, dog, goat, cow and eventually a horse, which killed her.

This is more or less, in mythic form, the story of what happens when you introduce one species in the hopes of keeping another one under control.

Take the Australian cane toad. In 1935, 101 cane toads were introduced to Australia in the hopes that they'd eat a particular sort of beetle that was a pest in the sugar cane crop. They are now a much bigger pest than any beetle.

Six months later there were 60,000 of them. There are now more than 200 million of them in the wild. Cane toads can lay 30,000 poisonous eggs at a time, and the eggs will grow into breathing, hopping pests within two weeks, and start breeding in a year. They can reach two kilograms in weight, have few natural predators, and among their favourite foods are honey bees. The Australian authorities are still trying to figure out, unsuccessfully, how to keep their numbers down.

Then there's Macquarie Island – a fifty-square-mile piece of land halfway between Australia and Antarctica. Home to seals and penguins, it was declared a World Heritage Site in 1997.

By early 2009, it faced what scientists called a 'complete ecosystem meltdown'. The trouble started shortly after the island was first discovered, in 1810.

The arrival of ships brought rats and mice, which in the absence of predators bred like rabbits and threatened to overrun the island. So a few years later, cats were introduced. This helped to keep down the rats and mice for a bit – but then the island suffered a plague of feral cats, who made short work of two native species of bird life.

The sailors also introduced rabbits, in the hopes of establishing a ready food supply for humans. The rabbits, too, bred like rabbits: by the late twentieth century there were 130,000 of them – 2,600 per square mile. They soon threatened to strip the entire island of vegetation.

In 1968, therefore, in order to control the rabbits, scientists introduced myxomatosis and the European rabbit flea. This succeeded in killing off most of the rabbits – but in so doing, it deprived the feral cat population of one of its vital sources of food.

So the cats went back to eating the birds, killing 60,000 a year. This was a catastrophe. A programme was launched to exterminate the feral cats. By 2000, it had been successful. Which meant that the rabbits, mice and rats once again had no predators. Despite the myxomatosis, the rabbit population rallied impressively.

Some 40 per cent of the island has now been completely stripped of vegetation, and in 2006 the rabbits caused a landslide that wiped out a penguin colony.

So now – in a last-ditch rescue attempt which will cost more than £10 million and take an estimated seven years – ecologists are trying to kill every last rabbit, rat and mouse on the island to bring it safely back to square one.

The moral of the story is: don't swallow the fly in the first place.

* * *

Wendy Northcutt's first collection of *Darwin Awards* reproduces a letter from a physics student identified only as 'Michael', which seems to suggest that not only can your memory play tricks on you, it can play practical jokes.

Michael knew that it's perfectly possible to handle liquid nitrogen, despite its being around –200°C, because of something called the Leidenfrost effect; the rapid evaporation of the liquid caused by the heat from your skin will give it a cushion of gas that prevents it making physical contact.

When trying to impress some younger students, he told

them that it was even possible to swallow the stuff without harm – as he knew fine well from his days in a cryonics laboratory when they had amused themselves doing just that.

They seemed unconvinced. He resolved to show them.

'I unhesitatingly poured myself a glass and took a shot. Simple. Swallow, blow smoke out my nose, impress everyone,' wrote Michael. 'Within two seconds, I collapsed to the floor, unable to breathe or indeed do anything except feel intense pain.'

What he had (mis)remembered doing, he later had occasion to reflect, was holding it in his mouth to blow smoke rings. Swallowing it was a different matter. Trapped in his digestive tract, the gas expanded at great speed, crushing one of his lungs and burning him from the top of his throat to the bottom of his stomach.

Eight weeks later, he reported cheerily, he was 'virtually healed except for a number of unsightly scars'.

* * *

In summer 1993, Garry Hoy – a lawyer in the Toronto law firm of Holden Day Wilson – was commiserating with visiting law students about the fact that the windows of his offices wouldn't open on a hot day.

Look how strong they are, he said, running against one of them with his shoulder. It popped cleanly out from its frame, and he fell twenty-four floors to his death.

A policeman afterwards explained to reporters that Mr Hoy had been 'showing his knowledge of the tensile strength of window glass'.

* * *

The death of Sir Francis Bacon – not the drunk painter but the Renaissance essayist and author, if you believe some people, of the plays attributed to William Shakespeare – is a warning to us all of the dangers of scientific curiosity. Or, as John Aubrey put it in *Brief Lives*: 'Mr Hobbes told me that the cause of his lordship's death was trying an experiment.'

He had been taking the air in his coach in the winter of 1626, on the way to Highgate, and observed the snow lying thickly about him on the ground. Was it the whiteness, or the powderiness, or some instinctive understanding of the metabolic behaviour of yet-to-be-discovered bacteria that set him thinking? We shall never know. But he shared his thoughts with his companion Dr Winterborne, physician to the king.

'It came into my Lord's thoughts why flesh might not be preserved in snow, as in salt,' reports Aubrey. 'They resolved to try the experiment presently. They alighted out of the coach and went into a poor woman's house at the bottom of Highgate Hill [it will be of no moment to the reader, though it weighs on me heavily, that this tragic drama played itself out right round the corner from my house], and bought a hen, and made the woman exenterate it, and then stuffed the body with snow, and my Lord did help to do it himself.'

At this point, Bacon had invented the frozen chicken four hundred years before Clarence Birdseye. His luck did not hold, however: 'The snow so chilled him that he immediately fell so extremely ill that he could not return to his lodgings.'

He was taken instead up the hill to the Earl of Arundel's house, put in a damp old bed, and within three days was stone dead.

Nobody knows what happened to the chicken. As we now

know, Birdseye got the credit for frozen food, just like Shakespeare did for the plays. Makes you wonder why anyone bothers, doesn't it?

* * *

A lady introduced to the nineteenth-century philosopher Herbert Spencer found herself at his side during mealtimes for three days running. He didn't speak a word. On the fourth day, he removed two pads of cotton wool from his ears. 'I stop my ears with these,' he told her solemnly, 'when I perceive there is no one at the table likely to afford rational conversation.' He replaced them.

* * *

The late Sir John Mortimer once profiled Kingsley Amis in *The Sunday Times*. Among the inaccuracies in his article were the claim that Amis had 'hit his son with a hammer'. Amis in fact said he'd hit his thumb with a hammer.

In similar vein, Sir Tom Stoppard once wrote to the *Guardian* to correct a mistake in an admiring profile of him. The author of the piece solemnly advised his readers that Stoppard's work had been informed by 'the Beckettian view that "I am a human nothing"'. Stoppard wrote to explain that, thirty years previously, he'd been misheard. He had actually said: 'I am assuming nothing.'

Ever since *The Times* of London in the nineteenth century reported, apocryphally, that Queen Victoria had pissed over London Bridge, the accidental mishearing has been one of the most important weapons in the journalist's armoury. A diarist for the *Evening Standard* named Harry Phibbs – now a distinguished member of Hammersmith and

Fulham Borough Council – was a master of the art. I once met Norman, now Lord Lamont, at a party. He gestured over at Phibbs.

'I hate that man!' he said. 'Do you know what he did to me? I was at a party for Richard Whiteley (late host of *Countdown*), and he asked me what I was doing there. I said that I'd always been a great admirer of Richard Whiteley's ties.'

Phibbs had gone away and written in the paper, apparently, that the former Chancellor of the Exchequer was 'a great admirer of Richard Whiteley's thighs'.

* * *

One of the most influential intellectual works of the twentieth century was *Principia Mathematica*, a three-volume treatise on the foundations of mathematics by Bertrand Russell and Alfred North Whitehead. It is widely regarded as being the most important work on the subject since Aristotle.

As Russell recalled in his autobiography, the manuscript was of a nature that meant it could not be typed or copied, so the authors had to prepare it for publication by hand. It weighed so much they had to hire an old four-wheel cart to lug it to the University Press.

When they got there, they learned that the University Press had estimated that publishing the book would make them a £600 loss. That was twice as much as the University Press was prepared to shoulder. Of the remaining £300, the Royal Society donated £200, and the authors had to club together and pay the final £100 from their own pockets.

'We thus earned minus £50 each by ten years work,' wrote Russell. 'This beats the record of *Paradise Lost*.'

* * *

<Patrician|Away>: what does your robot do, sam
<bovril>: it collects data about the surrounding environment,
then discards it and drives into walls

(Fragmentary transcript from an Internet chat room,
archived at www.bash.org)

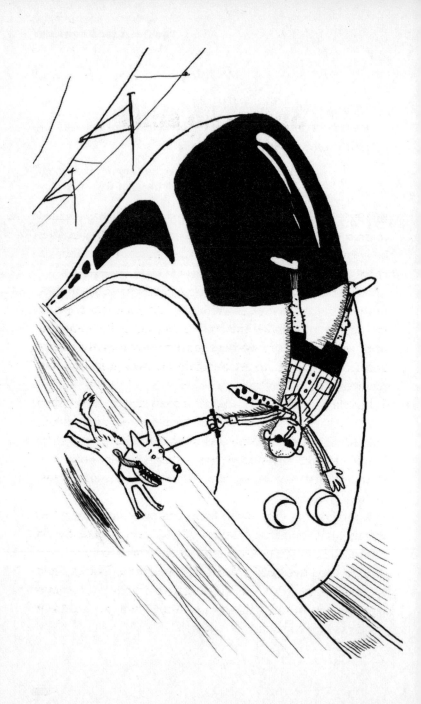

ODDS AND SODS

In 1995, Tom and Trixie Cummins of Austin, Texas decided to do something to help homeless people in their area after being reduced to tears by a local television report about a canned food drive.

'We'd had a few drinks and immediately started gathering most of the tins we had in the kitchen, drove them down to the depot, and handed them over. I'd forgotten all about it until yesterday, when we were getting ready for a toga party and Trixie asked me to get her diamond necklace,' Tom told reporters.

'I picked up the fake Campbell's soup can where we keep our valuables and tried to open it. I couldn't twist the top off, but at first I just thought it was rusty, so I used a can opener to open the lid. But inside there was only Scotch broth.

'I remember saying to Trixie "I don't feel too good" just before I passed out.'

Although the Campbell's Soup company volunteered to match Mr Cummins's offer of $2,500 as a reward for its return, the can full of jewellery was never recovered.

'One good deed and I'm over $70,000 out of pocket,' said Mr Cummins, who was cautioned by police for spray-painting the words 'Robbing Cheating Scum' on the front windows of his insurance company.

* * *

History did not cut Oedipus the break he might reasonably have hoped for. Foundation stone of the Western drama and plughole of the Western mind, Oedipus is the original demonstration of Sod's Law in action.

It starts with the oracle. Not so Delphic on this particular occasion, it tells King Laius of Thebes in no uncertain terms that he's 'doomed to die at the hands of his own son'. So Laius arranges for his son to be killed, as a precautionary measure. Long story short, the kid isn't killed. In fact, after passing through the hands of two random shepherds, he's adopted by the royal family of Corinth.

When he's a teenager, Oedipus himself consults the oracle, which announces that he's fated to kill his father and sleep with his mother. Mortified, Oedipus flees the city – and straightaway gets involved in a road-rage incident with a stranger.

The argument escalates, and Oedipus kills the other man. Who – of all the wretched coincidences – turns out to be none other than King Laius. Oblivious of this, Oedipus ambles on and after seeing off the Sphinx – which has been terrorizing Thebes with its irritating riddles – is offered the crown of Thebes and the hand of the attractive, widowed Jocasta. Who is, wouldn't you know it, his mum.

None of this would have come to light, however, were it not for the fact that Sod's Law dictated that not only did Oedipus kill his father and marry his mother, but that of all the shepherds in all the sheepfolds in the ancient world, the two best able to cast unwelcome light on the saga show up in quick succession.

A messenger arrives from Corinth to announce that the King has died of natural causes. Hooray, thinks Oedipus. That's that half of the prophecy thwarted. But by an astonishing coincidence, this messenger was, in a former life, none other than the shepherd who arranged his adoption. Not to worry about the incest bit coming true, he pipes up, Merope – the Queen of Corinth – wasn't his real mother anyway.

On he burbles. He was the one who brought baby Oedipus to Corinth, see, having been entrusted with the child by this other shepherd, who had it in the first place from the royal house of Thebes.

Jocasta turns green and goes inside to lie down. Oedipus, meanwhile, is still putting it together. Where can this other shepherd be found, then? Oedipus wonders aloud. Once again, Sod intervenes. It so happens he's already been sent for. For the self-same shepherd who had been entrusted to get rid of Oedipus happens to be the sole witness to the killing of King Laius. Small world.

Up he duly turns, the whole grisly plot unravels, Jocasta tops herself, and Oedipus loses his mind and strikes out his eyes. Those whom the sods wish to destroy, as every schoolboy knows, they first make mad.

* * *

After inheriting £20,000,000 at the age of 35, former pest control officer Stuart Holzman bought a new speedboat, crewed it with four nude models, and drove it up and down in front of Bimini Marina in the Bahamas, scattering $100 bills into the water. Four people drowned trying to retrieve the money.

* * *

As befits the author of *Oedipus Rex*, Sophocles died in a manner that will surely have left his shade kicking itself in the Elysian Fields. When Sophocles was 90 – an almost superhuman degree of longevity for the ancient world – his son Iophon took him to court. Iophon – no doubt, like Prince Charles, fed up of waiting for his inheritance – insisted that Sophocles was gaga, and no longer capable of running his own affairs.

Sophocles saw him off. He recited a chunk of *Oedipus at Colonus*. 'If I am Sophocles, I am not senile,' he declared. 'And if I am senile, I am not Sophocles.' So baffled was the court by this that they dismissed the case.

Delighted by his triumph, the old boy attempted a sort of victory lap in the form of a public reading of *Antigone*. In the course of that, he tried to get a particularly long sentence out in a single breath and expired on the spot.

His brother playwrights fared little better. Euripides died when, during the course of a lovers's tiff, his girlfriend set a pack of wild dogs on him and they ripped him limb from limb. Aeschylus, at the ripe old age of 68, was on holiday in Sicily when a tortoise dropped out of the sky, hit him on the head and killed him stone dead. An eagle, apparently, mistook his bald head for the sort of rock on which you could crack open a tortoise.

Sic transit gloria mundi, as the three Greeks would not have said.

* * *

A guide dog in Wuppertal, Germany, was judged by its trainer to be in need of 'a brush-up on some elementary skills' after killing four of its owners in a row. The dog's name was 'Lucky'.

'I admit it's not an impressive record on paper,' Ernst Gerber said. 'He led his first owner in front of a moving bus, and the second off the end of a pier. He actually pushed the third owner off a railway platform just as the Cologne to Frankfurt express was approaching, and he walked his fourth owner into heavy traffic, before abandoning him and running away to safety. But apart from the epileptic fits, he has a lovely temperament.'

* * *

Two men. A windswept promontory. A question of honour. The crack of pistols. One man falls. Another man walks away, sadder but wiser.

That's how duels are supposed to go: dramatic, romantic, lip-tremblingly noble and sexy. It is not, however, how the face-off between the Irish poet Thomas Moore (a friend of Byron but not, evidently, one ever destined to enjoy the same afterlife as an adjective) and the critic Francis Jeffrey played itself out.

At issue was a review of Moore's poems that Jeffrey had written for the *Edinburgh Review*, in which he described the verse as 'a tissue of sick and fantastical conceits', and the author as a scoundrel: 'the most licentious of modern versifiers and the most poetical of those who in our time have devoted themselves to the propagation of immorality'.

Moore resolved to demand satisfaction. Then decided he couldn't afford the train fare to Edinburgh, so gave up. Then he heard that Jeffrey was, in fact, in London after all. The spirit of Nemesis stirred in him again, and tracking down his quarry, he issued the challenge.

Duels aren't as easy to organize as they might sound, however. These milquetoast literary men were just at a scratch able to secure the services of a second – Moore managed to talk his friend Dr Thomas Hume into the role, whereas Jeffrey twisted the arm of one Francis Horner.

But neither owned a pistol. Moore eventually managed to borrow a pair from a friend. At last, with dawn breaking over Chalk Farm in north London, the scene was set for bloody vengeance.

Until it turned out that Horner had not the first idea how to load a pistol. After much kerfuffle, the loading of Jeffrey's pistol was entrusted to his opponent's second. A gamble, you might think, but by the time all this faffing about was over, Moore had said something agreeable about the weather, and the sworn enemies had fallen into friendly conversation.

Nevertheless, honour needed to be satisfied. Both men took the requisite three paces, raised their weapons, and... the police jumped out of the bushes and placed them under arrest. The owner of the pistols – and here, I conjecture, he was simply trying to save these boobies the embarrassment of going through with the duel – had been indiscreet about the duel, causing someone to tip off the filth.

As the two combatants were detained in Bow Street magistrate's court awaiting bail, however, they chattered away about books. A firm friendship was clearly blossoming – so firm, in fact, that it survived the discovery that Moore's pistol had been loaded but that Jeffrey's (loaded, we'll remember, by Moore's second) didn't have a bullet in it. Hume was by this stage so embarrassed by the whole affair that he refused to put his name to a written explanation of what had happened, and a newspaper report put the tin hat on the whole affair by misprinting 'pellet' for 'bullet'.

Jeffrey and Moore were firm friends for the rest of their days.

* * *

Mithridates the Great, who ruled an area of what's now northern Turkey in the first century BC, was a formidable enemy of the Roman Empire: a last holdout of Old Greece against New Rome.

As befitted a man in his position, he was paranoid as all hell. Not trusting human guards alone, he is said to have posted at his bedside a horse, a bull and a stag – a trio of animals wisely chosen to be likely to make a helpful stampeding noise when approached by assassins, but not to fancy mating with each other in a way that might disturb the Mithridatic repose.

Poison, though, was his big worry. Convinced that his enemies would seek to kill him off with some toxic substance or other, he set about building up an immunity by taking ever greater non-lethal doses of specific poisons, in addition to a daily glug of a universal antidote of his own devising, which consisted according to the Roman encyclopaedist Celsus of:

> ... costmary 1.66 grams, sweet flag 20 grams, hypericum, gum, sagapenum, acacia juice, Illyrian iris, cardamon, 8 grams each, anise 12 grams, Gallic nard, gentian root and dried rose-leaves, 16 grams each, poppy-tears and parsley, 17 grams each, casia, saxifrage, darnel, long pepper, 20.66 grams each, storax 21 grams, castoreum, frankincense, hypocistis juice, myrrh and opopanax, 24 grams each, malabathrum leaves 24 grams, flower of round rush, turpentine-resin, galbanum, Cretan carrot seeds, 24.66 grams each, nard and opobalsam, 25 grams each, shepherd's purse 25 grams, rhubarb root 28 grams, saffron, ginger, cinnamon, 29 grams each. These are pounded and taken up in honey.

This is roughly, I think, what they now make Fisherman's Friends out of. In any case, it worked. As A. E. Housman later hymned it: 'They put arsenic in his meat/ And stared aghast to watch him eat; They poured strychnine in his cup/ And shook to see him drink it up'.

Mithridates's luck eventually ran out, though. In 65 BC his forces were routed by Pompey's Roman army. Rather than be captured and led in ignominy through the streets of Rome, he made to do away with himself.

He drank a mighty draught of poison, which – of course – completely failed to work. Sick as a dog, but quite alive, Mithridates was forced to call in a favour from a Gaulish pal, who obligingly hacked him to death.

* * *

Killing yourself by jumping off a tall building is a project positively fraught with hazards. Quite aside from the antisocial consequences of your likely landing, the historical record includes several instances of jumpers being thwarted by rogue gusts of wind.

One such was 26-year-old Hawaiian Thomas Helms, who in December 1977 leapt from the observation deck on the 86th floor of the Empire State Building only to land on a ledge twenty feet below. Knocked silly, he was dragged inside by rescuers.

NBC television put him on air immediately. He told them that he had had second thoughts about killing himself immediately after he jumped.

A yet more bathetic attempt at suicide by gravity is instanced by the story – persistent though likely apocryphal – about the miserable janitor who ties the cable of his industrial floor-polisher around his neck and throws it off a 100-foot roof.

Being an industrial floor polisher, its cable is 150 feet long.

It smashes into the ground and our demoralized would-be-statistic is billed for its replacement.

* * *

When the London publisher John Hotten bounced a cheque on the American journalist Ambrose Bierce, Bierce was determined 'to have Hotten's blood'. Bierce first laid siege to Hotten's offices in Piccadilly – and on discovering that Hotten hadn't been seen there for several days, bullied a clerk into giving him the publisher's home address: 4, Maitland Park Villas, Haverstock Hill.

There, hot with rage, he presented himself that very afternoon with the returned cheque in his pocket. 'Where's Mr Hotten?' he asked the maid who answered the door.

'Come this way, sir,' she said. 'I'll take you to him.'

She ushered him into the darkened room where Hotten was lying in bed. 'What the hell's the meaning of this, Hotten?' demanded Bierce, pulling the cheque from his pocket and waving it in his face.

Answer came there none. Hotten was dead. The maid had thought Bierce was the undertaker.

* * *

A friend of mine was in a trendy Shoreditch taxidermist recently, and told the woman behind the counter that he was thinking of having a beloved parrot stuffed when he died.

'So the woman looks at me all serious, and asks her husband to join us, and gets us a seat and we discuss the process. She explains, needlessly I think, that it's legal in some countries.

'I say sure. And she asks about pose. And I say a natural one. She offers to maybe gild the nails, and has some exciting ideas for eyes. She asks how my mother feels about it. I say fine. She asks how old he is. I say 23. She says: "Your father is 23?" No. But my parrot is. She thought I'd said I wanted to have my beloved PARENT stuffed.'

I wonder about the truth of this story, but my friend swears blind to it, and I feel obliged to believe him.

* * *

In 1989 a New York wine merchant named William Sokolin was in possession of a bottle of Château Margaux 1787 which had once belonged to Thomas Jefferson. He took it to a dinner for wine aficionados at the Four Seasons restaurant in Manhattan, in the hopes of drumming up publicity for the sale of the bottle. He was asking half a million dollars for it. At the end of the evening, a waiter carrying a tray of coffee knocked the bottle over and broke it. The insurance company paid out $225,000.

* * *

Courtesy, taken too far, invariably backfires. Witness thus the crisp exchange of greetings between the seventeenth-century scholar Isaac Barrow, and the rakehell poet Lord Rochester – each of whom cordially hated the other – when they bumped into each other at court.

   Rochester: 'Doctor – I am yours to my shoe tie.'
   Barrow: 'My lord, I am yours to the ground.'
   Rochester: 'Doctor, I am yours to the centre.'
   Barrow: 'My lord, I am yours to the antipodes.'

Rochester: 'Doctor, I am yours to the lowest pit of hell!'
Barrow [turning on his heel]: 'There, my lord, I leave you.'

* * *

P. G. Wodehouse came under attack in the public prints from a correspondent with the pen-name 'Indignant', who complained that Wodehouse's writing was badly overrated.

Wodehouse was stung into a public response. In his 1967 book *Over Seventy*, he directed 'Indignant's' attention to a letter to *The Times* from a Mr Verrier Elwin of Patangarth, India. Mr Elwin's letter described how a cow had wandered into his home and eaten his copy of *Carry On, Jeeves*, selecting it from a shelf which contained, among other works, books by Galsworthy, Jane Austen and T. S. Eliot. 'Surely a rather striking tribute.'

* * *

Nathanael West, author of *Miss Lonelyhearts* and *The Day of the Locust*, was once warned by one of the many friends who refused to climb in a car with him that unless he looked where he was going when driving, 'someday he would be killed'. West, renowned for his capricious U-turns across six lanes of oncoming traffic, poor eyesight and history of crashes, laughed in his friend's face.

In December 1940, he roared through a red light on the way back from a hunting weekend in Mexico and crashed into the first oncoming car, killing himself and Mrs West.

West got the last laugh on his friend, however. He had been looking where he was going. Unfortunately, he suffered from red–green colour-blindness.

* * *

When Jane Birkin's mum went to visit her in Paris, the eccentric English actress and chanteuse – who was due to be out filming – told her to let herself into the apartment and make herself at home. The door was locked by an electronic keypad and the code, she said, was the year of Birkin's birth.

Birkin arrived back hours later to find her mother stranded, with her luggage, on the pavement in the pouring rain. 'Oh my God!' she remembered. 'I forgot to tell you. I lied to the doorknob about my age.'

* * *

An old friend of mine whose face tends to relax into an expression of gloom was reproved as a child by an elderly lady. 'Cheer up,' she said. 'It might never happen.'

He looked her up and down. 'It happened to you, didn't it?'